THE LITERATURE OF
DEATH AND DYING

DEATH AS A SPECULATIVE THEME
IN RELIGIOUS, SCIENTIFIC,
AND SOCIAL THOUGHT

ARNO PRESS

A New York Times Company

New York / 1977

Reprint Edition 1977 by Arno Press Inc.

Copyright © 1977 by Arno Press Inc.

The Question of Brotherhood was reprinted
by permission of Quadrangle/The New York
Times Book Company, Inc.

THE LITERATURE OF DEATH AND DYING
ISBN for complete set: 0-405-09550-3
See last pages of this volume for titles.

Manufactured in the United States of America

Publisher's Note: The articles in this
anthology have been reprinted from the
best available copies.

————◆————

Library of Congress Cataloging in Publication Data
Main entry under title:

Death as a speculative theme in religious, scientific,
    and social thought.

    (The Literature of death and dying)
    1. Death--Addresses, essays, lectures. I. Series.
BD444.D37   128'.5   76-19566
ISBN 0-405-09562-7

CONTENTS

George, Henry, THE CURRENT THEORY OF HUMAN
PROGRESS—ITS INSUFFICIENCY. (Reprinted from *Progress
and Poverty*, 50th Anniversary Edition, pp. 475-488).
New York, 1929

George, Henry, THE CENTRAL TRUTH. (Reprinted from
Progress and Poverty, 50th Anniversary Edition, pp. 544-552).
New York, 1929

George, Henry, THE PROBLEM OF INDIVIDUAL LIFE.
(Reprinted from *Progress and Poverty*, 50th Anniversary Edition,
pp. 555-565). New York, 1929

Reade, [William] Winwood, THE FUTURE OF THE HUMAN
RACE and THE RELIGION OF REASON AND LOVE. (Reprinted
from *The Martyrdom of Man*, Sixteenth Edition, pp. 502-543).
New York, 1908

Fyodorov, Nicholas, THE QUESTION OF BROTHERHOOD OR
RELATEDNESS, AND OF THE REASONS FOR THE UN-
BROTHERLY, DIS-RELATED, OR UNPEACEFUL STATE OF THE
WORLD, AND OF THE MEANS FOR THE RESTORATION
OF RELATEDNESS. [1906]

Berdyaev, Nicholas, THE ESCHATOLOGICAL AND PROPHETIC
CHARACTER OF RUSSIAN THOUGHT. (Reprinted from *The
Russian Idea*, pp. 193-218). New York, 1948

Berdyaev, Nicholas, DEATH AND IMMORTALITY. (Reprinted
from *The Destiny of Man*, pp. 317-337). London, 1937

Needham, Joseph, SCIENCE, RELIGION AND SOCIALISM.
(Reprinted from *Time: The Refreshing River*, pp. 42-74).
New York, 1943

THE CURRENT THEORY
OF HUMAN PROGRESS —
ITS INSUFFICIENCY

Henry George

What in me is dark
Illumine, what is low raise and support;
That to the height of this great argument
I may assert eternal Providence
And justify the ways of God to men.
                    —*Milton.*

If the conclusions at which we have arrived are correct, they will fall under a larger generalization.

Let us, therefore, recommence our inquiry from a higher standpoint, whence we may survey a wider field.

What is the law of human progress?

This is a question which, were it not for what has gone before, I should hesitate to review in the brief space I can now devote to it, as it involves, directly or indirectly, some of the very highest problems with which the human mind can engage. But it is a question which naturally comes up. Are or are not the conclusions to which we have come consistent with the great law under which human development goes on?

What is that law? We must find the answer to our question; for the current philosophy, though it clearly recognizes the existence of such a law, gives no more satisfactory account of it than the current political economy does of the persistence of want amid advancing wealth.

Let us, as far as possible, keep to the firm ground of facts. Whether man was or was not gradually developed from an animal, it is not necessary to inquire. However intimate may be the connection between questions which relate to man as we know him and questions which relate to his genesis, it is only from the former upon the latter that light can be thrown. Inference cannot proceed from the unknown to the known. It is only from facts of which we are cognizant that we can infer what has preceded cognizance.

However man may have originated, all we know of him is as man—just as he is now to be found. There is no record or trace of him in any lower condition than that in which savages are still to be met. By whatever bridge he may have crossed the wide chasm which now separates him from the brutes, there remain of it no vestiges. Between the lowest savages of whom we know and the highest animals, there is an irreconcilable difference—a difference not merely of degree, but of kind. Many of the characteristics, actions, and emotions of man are exhibited by the lower animals; but man, no matter how low in the scale of humanity, has never yet been found destitute of one thing of which no animal shows the slightest trace, a clearly recognizable but almost undefinable something, which gives him the power of improvement—which makes him the progressive animal.

The beaver builds a dam, and the bird a nest, and the bee a cell; but while beavers' dams, and birds' nests, and bees' cells are always constructed on the same model, the house of the man passes from the rude hut of leaves and branches to the magnificent mansion replete with modern conveniences. The dog can to a certain extent connect cause and effect, and may be taught some tricks; but his capacity in these respects has not been a whit increased during all the ages he has been the associate of improving man, and the dog of civilization is not a whit more accomplished or intelligent than the dog of the wandering savage. We know of no animal that uses clothes, that cooks its food, that makes itself tools or weapons, that breeds other animals that it wishes to eat, or that has an articulate language. But men who do not do such things have never yet been found, or heard of, except in fable. That is to say, man, wherever we know him, exhibits this power—of supplementing what nature has done for him by what he does for himself; and, in fact, so inferior is the physical endowment of man, that there is no part of the world, save perhaps some of the small islands of the Pacific, where without this faculty he could maintain an existence.

Man everywhere and at all times exhibits this faculty —everywhere and at all times of which we have knowledge he has made some use of it. But the degree in which this has been done greatly varies. Between the rude canoe and the steamship; between the boomerang and the repeating rifle; between the roughly carved wooden idol and the breathing marble of Grecian art; between savage knowledge and modern science; between the wild Indian and the white settler; between the Hottentot woman and the belle of polished society, there is an enormous difference.

The varying degrees in which this faculty is used cannot be ascribed to differences in original capacity—the most highly improved peoples of the present day were savages within historic times, and we meet with the widest differences between peoples of the same stock. Nor can they be wholly ascribed to differences in physical environment—the cradles of learning and the arts are now in many cases tenanted by barbarians, and within a few years great cities rise on the hunting grounds of wild tribes. All these differences are evidently connected with social development. Beyond perhaps the veriest rudiments, it becomes possible for man to improve only as he lives with his fellows. All these improvements, therefore, in man's powers and conditions we summarize in the term civilization. Men improve as they become civilized, or learn to co-operate in society.

What is the law of this improvement? By what common principle can we explain the different stages of civilization at which different communities have arrived? In what consists essentially the progress of civilization, so that we may say of varying social adjustments, this favors it, and that does not; or explain why an institution or condition which may at one time advance it may at another time retard it?

The prevailing belief now is, that the progress of civilization is a development or evolution, in the course of which man's powers are increased and his qualities improved by the operation of causes similar to those which are relied upon as explaining the genesis of species— viz., the survival of the fittest and the hereditary trans· mission of acquired qualities.

That civilization is an evolution—that it is, in the language of Herbert Spencer, a progress from an indefinite, incoherent homogeneity to a definite, coherent heterogeneity—there is no doubt; but to say this is not to explain or identify the causes which forward or retard it. How far the sweeping generalizations of Spencer, which seek to account for all phenomena under terms of matter and force, may, properly understood, include all these causes, I am unable to say; but, as scientifically expounded, the development philosophy has either not yet definitely met this question, or has given birth, or rather coherency, to an opinion which does not accord with the facts.

The vulgar explanation of progress is, I think, very much like the view naturally taken by the money maker of the causes of the unequal distribution of wealth. His theory, if he has one, usually is, that there is plenty of money to be made by those who have will and ability, and that it is ignorance, or idleness, or extravagance, that makes the difference between the rich and the poor. And so the common explanation of differences of civilization is of differences in capacity. The civilized races are the superior races, and advance in civilization is according to this superiority—just as English victories were, in common English opinion, due to the natural superiority of Englishmen to frog-eating Frenchmen; and popular government, active invention, and greater average comfort are, or were until lately, in common American opinion, due to the greater "smartness of the Yankee Nation."

Now, just as the politico-economic doctrines which in the beginning of this inquiry we met and disproved, harmonize with the common opinion of men who see capitalists paying wages and competition reducing wages; just as the Malthusian theory harmonized with existing prejudices both of the rich and the poor; so does the explanation of progress as a gradual race improvement harmonize with the vulgar opinion which accounts by race differences for differences in civilization. It has given coherence and a scientific formula to opinions which already prevailed. Its wonderful spread since the time Darwin first startled the world with his "Origin of Species" has not been so much a conquest as an assimilation.

The view which now dominates the world of thought is this: That the struggle for existence, just in proportion as it becomes intense, impels men to new efforts and inventions. That this improvement and capacity for improvement is fixed by hereditary transmission, and extended by the tendency of the best adapted individual, or most improved individual, to survive and propagate among individuals, and of the best adapted, or most improved tribe, nation, or race to survive in the struggle between social aggregates. On this theory the differences between man and the animals, and differences in the relative progress of men, are now explained as confidently, and all but as generally, as a little while ago they were explained upon the theory of special creation and divine interposition.

The practical outcome of this theory is in a sort of hopeful fatalism, of which current literature is full.* In this view, progress is the result of forces which work slowly, steadily, and remorselessly, for the elevation of man. War, slavery, tyranny, superstition, famine, and pestilence, the want and misery which fester in modern civilization, are the impelling causes which drive man on, by eliminating poorer types and extending the higher; and hereditary transmission is the power by which advances are fixed, and past advances made the footing for new advances. The individual is the result of changes thus impressed upon and perpetuated through a long series of past individuals, and the social organization takes its form from the individuals of which it is composed. Thus, while this theory is, as Herbert Spencer says†—"radical to a degree beyond anything which current radicalism conceives," inasmuch as it looks for changes in the very nature of man; it is at the same time "conservative to a degree beyond anything conceived by current conservatism," inasmuch as it holds that no change can avail save these slow changes in men's natures. Philosophers may teach that this does not lessen the duty of endeavoring to reform abuses,

---

* In semi-scientific or popularized form this may perhaps be seen in best, because frankest, expression in "The Martyrdom of Man," by Winwood Reade, a writer of singular vividness and power. This book is in reality a history of progress, or, rather, a monograph upon its causes and methods, and will well repay perusal for its vivid pictures, whatever may be thought of the capacity of the author for philosophic generalization. The connection between subject and title may be seen by the conclusion: "I give to universal history a strange but true title— *The Martyrdom of Man.* In each generation the human race has been tortured that their children might profit by their woes. Our own prosperity is founded on the agonies of the past. Is it therefore unjust that we also should suffer for the benefit of those who are to come?"

† "The Study of Sociology"—Conclusion.

just as the theologians who taught predestinarianism in-
sisted on the duty of all to struggle for salvation; but,
as generally apprehended, the result is fatalism—"do
what we may, the mills of the gods grind on regardless
either of our aid or our hindrance." I allude to this only
to illustrate what I take to be the opinion now rapidly
spreading and permeating common thought; not that in
the search for truth any regard for its ·effects should
be permitted to bias the mind. But this I take to be
the current view of civilization: That it is the result of
forces, operating in the way indicated, which slowly
change the character, and improve and elevate the powers of man; that the difference between civilized man
and savage is of a long race education, which has become permanently fixed in mental organization; and that
this improvement tends to go on increasingly, to a
higher and higher civilization. We have reached such
a point that progress seems to be natural with us, and
we look forward confidently to the greater achievements
of the coming race—some even holding that the progress
of science will finally give men immortality and enable
them to make bodily the tour not only of the planets,
but of the fixed stars, and at length to manufacture suns
and systems for themselves.*

But without soaring to the stars, the moment that
this theory of progression, which seems so natural to us
amid an advancing civilization, looks around the world,
it comes against an enormous fact—the fixed, petrified
civilizations. The majority of the human race to-day
have no idea of progress; the majority of the human race
to-day look (as until a few generations ago our own ancestors looked) upon the past as the time of human perfection. The difference between the savage and the
civilized man may be explained on the theory that the

---

* Winwood Reade, "The Martyrdom of Man."

former is as yet so imperfectly developed that his progress is hardly apparent; but how, upon the theory that
human progress is the result of general and continuous
causes, shall we account for the civilizations that have
progressed so far and then stopped? It cannot be said
of the Hindoo and of the Chinaman, as it may be said of
the savage, that our superiority is the result of a longer
education; that we are, as it were, the grown men of
nature, while they are the children. The Hindoos and
the Chinese were civilized when we were savages. They
had great cities, highly organized and powerful governments, literatures, philosophies, polished manners, considerable division of labor, large commerce, and elaborate
arts, when our ancestors were wandering barbarians,
living in huts and skin tents, not a whit further advanced than the American Indians. While we have progressed from this savage state to Nineteenth Century
civilization, they have stood still. If progress be the
result of fixed laws, inevitable and eternal, which impel
men forward, how shall we account for this?

One of the best popular expounders of the development philosophy, Walter Bagehot ("Physics and Politics"), admits the force of this objection, and endeavors
in this way to explain it: That the first thing necessary
to civilize man is to tame him; to induce him to live in
association with his fellows in subordination to law; and
hence a body or "cake" of laws and customs grows up,
being intensified and extended by natural selection, the
tribe or nation thus bound together having an advantage
over those who are not. That this cake of custom and
law finally becomes too thick and hard to permit further
progress, which can go on only as circumstances occur
which introduce discussion, and thus permit the freedom
and mobility necessary to improvement.

This explanation, which Mr. Bagehot offers, as he
says, with some misgivings, is I think at the expense of

the general theory. But it is not worth while speaking of that, for it, manifestly, does not explain the facts.

The hardening tendency of which Mr. Bagehot speaks would show itself at a very early period of development, and his illustrations of it are nearly all drawn from savage or semi-savage life. Whereas, these arrested civilizations had gone a long distance before they stopped. There must have been a time when they were very far advanced as compared with the savage state, and were yet plastic, free, and advancing. These arrested civilizations stopped at a point which was hardly in anything inferior and in many respects superior to European civilization of, say, the sixteenth or at any rate the fifteenth century. Up to that point then there must have been discussion, the hailing of what was new, and mental activity of all sorts. They had architects who carried the art of building, necessarily by a series of innovations or improvements, up to a very high point; ship-builders who in the same way, by innovation after innovation, finally produced as good a vessel as the war ships of Henry VIII; inventors who stopped only on the verge of our most important improvements, and from some of whom we can yet learn; engineers who constructed great irrigation works and navigable canals; rival schools of philosophy and conflicting ideas of religion. One great religion, in many respects resembling Christianity, rose in India, displaced the old religion, passed into China, sweeping over that country, and was displaced again in its old seats, just as Christianity was displaced in its first seats. There was life, and active life, and the innovation that begets improvement, long after men had learned to live together. And, moreover, both India and China have received the infusion of new life in conquering races, with different customs and modes of thought.

The most fixed and petrified of all civilizations of

which we know anything was that of Egypt, where even art finally assumed a conventional and inflexible form. But we know that behind this must have been a time of life and vigor—a freshly developing and expanding civilization, such as ours is now—or the arts and sciences could never have been carried to such a pitch. And recent excavations have brought to light from beneath what we before knew of Egypt an earlier Egypt still—in statues and carvings which, instead of a hard and formal type, beam with life and expression, which show art struggling, ardent, natural, and free, the sure indication of an active and expanding life. So it must have been once with all now unprogressive civilizations.

But it is not merely these arrested civilizations that the current theory of development fails to account for. It is not merely that men have gone so far on the path of progress and then stopped; it is that men have gone far on the path of progress and then gone back. It is not merely an isolated case that thus confronts the theory—*it is the universal rule.* Every civilization that the world has yet seen has had its period of vigorous growth, of arrest and stagnation; its decline and fall. Of all the civilizations that have arisen and flourished, there remain to-day but those that have been arrested, and our own, which is not yet as old as were the pyramids when Abraham looked upon them—while behind the pyramids were twenty centuries of recorded history.

That our own civilization has a broader base, is of a more advanced type, moves quicker and soars higher than any preceding civilization is undoubtedly true; but in these respects it is hardly more in advance of the Greco-Roman civilization than that was in advance of Asiatic civilization; and if it were, that would prove nothing as to its permanence and future advance, unless it be shown that it is superior in those things which caused the ultimate failure of its predecessors. The current theory does not assume this.

In truth, nothing could be further from explaining the facts of universal history than this theory that civilization is the result of a course of natural selection which operates to improve and elevate the powers of man. That civilization has arisen at different times in different places and has progressed at different rates, is not inconsistent with this theory; for that might result from the unequal balancing of impelling and resisting forces; but that progress everywhere commencing, for even among the lowest tribes it is held that there has been some progress, has nowhere been continuous, but has everywhere been brought to a stand or retrogression, *is* absolutely inconsistent. For if progress operated to fix an improvement in man's nature and thus to produce further progress, though there might be occasional interruption, yet the general rule would be that progress would be continuous—that advance would lead to advance, and civilization develop into higher civilization.

Not merely the general rule, but *the universal rule,* is the reverse of this. The earth is the tomb of the dead empires, no less than of dead men. Instead of progress fitting men for greater progress, every civilization that was in its own time as vigorous and advancing as ours is now, has of itself come to a stop. Over and over again, art has declined, learning sunk, power waned, population become sparse, until the people who had built great temples and mighty cities, turned rivers and pierced mountains, cultivated the earth like a garden and introduced the utmost refinement into the minute affairs of life, remained but in a remnant of squalid barbarians, who had lost even the memory of what their ancestors had done, and regarded the surviving fragments of their grandeur as the work of genii, or of the mighty race before the flood. So true is this, that when we think of the past, it seems like the inexorable law, from which we can no more hope to be exempt than the young man who "feels his life in every limb" can hope to be exempt from the dissolution which is the common fate of all. "Even this, O Rome, must one day be thy fate!" wept Scipio over the ruins of Carthage, and Macaulay's picture of the New Zealander musing upon the broken arch of London Bridge appeals to the imagination of even those who see cities rising in the wilderness and help to lay the foundations of new empire. And so, when we erect a public building we make a hollow in the largest corner stone and carefully seal within it some mementos of our day, looking forward to the time when our works shall be ruins and ourselves forgot.

Nor whether this alternate rise and fall of civilization, this retrogression that always follows progression, be, or be not, the rhythmic movement of an ascending line (and I think, though I will not open the question, that it would be much more difficult to prove the affirmative than is generally supposed) makes no difference; for the current theory is in either case disproved. Civilizations have died and made no sign, and hard-won progress has been lost to the race forever; but, even if it be admitted that each wave of progress has made possible a higher wave and each civilization passed the torch to a greater civilization, the theory that civilization advances by changes wrought in the nature of man fails to explain the facts; for in every case it is not the race that has been educated and hereditarily modified by the old civilization that begins the new, but a fresh race coming from a lower level. It is the barbarians of the one epoch who have been the civilized men of the next; to be in their turn succeeded by fresh barbarians. For it has been heretofore always the case that men under the influences of civilization, though at first improving, afterward degenerate. The civilized man of to-day is vastly the superior of the uncivilized; but so in the time of its vigor was the civilized man of every dead civilization. But there are such things as the vices, the corruptions, the enervations of civilization, which past a certain point have always heretofore shown themselves. Every civilization that has been overwhelmed by barbarians has really perished from internal decay.

This universal fact, the moment that it is recognized, disposes of the theory that progress is by hereditary transmission. Looking over the history of the world, the line of greatest advance does not coincide for any length of time with any line of heredity. On any particular line of heredity, retrogression seems always to follow advance.

Shall we therefore say that there is a national or race life, as there is an individual life—that every social aggregate has, as it were, a certain amount of energy, the expenditure of which necessitates decay? This is an old and widespread idea, that is yet largely held, and that may be constantly seen cropping out incongruously in the writings of the expounders of the development philosophy. Indeed, I do not see why it may not be stated in terms of matter and of motion so as to bring it clearly within the generalization of evolution. For considering its individuals as atoms, the growth of society is "an integration of matter and concomitant dissipation of motion; during which the matter passes from an indefinite, incoherent homogeneity to a definite, coherent heterogeneity, and during which the retained motion undergoes a parallel transformation." * And thus an analogy may be drawn between the life of a society and the life of a solar system upon the nebular hypothesis. As the heat and light of the sun are produced by the

---

* Herbert Spencer's definition of Evolution, "First Principles," p. 396.

aggregation of atoms evolving motion, which finally ceases when the atoms at length come to a state of equilibrium or rest, and a state of immobility succeeds, which can be broken in again only by the impact of external forces, which reverse the process of evolution, integrating motion and dissipating matter in the form of gas, again to evolve motion by its condensation; so, it may be said, does the aggregation of individuals in a community evolve a force which produces the light and warmth of civilization, but when this process ceases and the individual components are brought into a state of equilibrium, assuming their fixed places, petrifaction ensues, and the breaking up and diffusion caused by an incursion of barbarians is necessary to the recommencement of the process and a new growth of civilization.

But analogies are the most dangerous modes of thought. They may connect resemblances and yet disguise or cover up the truth. And all such analogies are superficial. While its members are constantly reproduced in all the fresh vigor of childhood, a community cannot grow old, as does a man, by the decay of its powers. While its aggregate force must be the sum of the forces of its individual components, a community cannot lose vital power unless the vital powers of its components are lessened.

Yet in both the common analogy which likens the life power of a nation to that of an individual, and in the one I have supposed, lurks the recognition of an obvious truth—the truth that the obstacles which finally bring progress to a halt are raised by the course of progress; that what has destroyed all previous civilizations has been the conditions produced by the growth of civilization itself.

This is a truth which in the current philosophy is ignored; but it is a truth most pregnant. Any valid theory of human progress must account for it.

THE CENTRAL TRUTH

Henry George

In the short space to which this latter part of our inquiry is necessarily confined, I have been obliged to omit much that I would like to say, and to touch briefly where an exhaustive consideration would not be out of place.

Nevertheless, this, at least, is evident, that the truth to which we were led in the politico-economic branch of our inquiry is as clearly apparent in the rise and fall of nations and the growth and decay of civilizations, and that it accords with those deep-seated recognitions of relation and sequence that we denominate moral perceptions. Thus have been given to our conclusions the greatest certitude and highest sanction.

This truth involves both a menace and a promise. It shows that the evils arising from the unjust and unequal distribution of wealth, which are becoming more and more apparent as modern civilization goes on, are not incidents of progress, but tendencies which must bring progress to a halt; that they will not cure themselves, but, on the contrary, must, unless their cause is removed, grow greater and greater, until they sweep us back into barbarism by the road every previous civilization has trod. But it also shows that these evils are not imposed by natural laws; that they spring solely from social maladjustments which ignore natural laws, and that in removing their cause we shall be giving an enormous impetus to progress.

The poverty which in the midst of abundance pinches and embrutes men, and all the manifold evils which flow from it, spring from a denial of justice. In permitting the monopolization of the opportunities which nature freely offers to all, we have ignored the fundamental law of justice—for, so far as we can see, when we view things upon a large scale, justice seems to be the supreme law of the universe. But by sweeping away this injustice and asserting the rights of all men to natural opportunities, we shall conform ourselves to the law—we shall remove the great cause of unnatural inequality in the distribution of wealth and power; we shall abolish poverty; tame the ruthless passions of greed; dry up the springs of vice and misery; light in dark places the lamp of knowledge; give new vigor to invention and a fresh impulse to discovery; substitute political strength for political weakness; and make tyranny and anarchy impossible.

The reform I have proposed accords with all that is politically, socially, or morally desirable. It has the qualities of a true reform, for it will make all other reforms easier. What is it but the carrying out in letter and spirit of the truth enunciated in the Declaration of Independence—the "self-evident" truth that is the heart and soul of the Declaration—*"That all men are created equal; that they are endowed by their Creator with certain unalienable rights; that among these are life, liberty, and the pursuit of happiness!"*

These rights are denied when the equal right to land —on which and by which men alone can live—is denied. Equality of political rights will not compensate for the denial of the equal right to the bounty of nature. Political liberty, when the equal right to land is denied, becomes, as population increases and invention goes on, merely the liberty to compete for employment at starvation wages. This is the truth that we have ignored.

And so there come beggars in our streets and tramps on our roads; and poverty enslaves men whom we boast are political sovereigns; and want breeds ignorance that our schools cannot enlighten; and citizens vote as their masters dictate; and the demagogue usurps the part of the statesman; and gold weighs in the scales of justice; and in high places sit those who do not pay to civic virtue even the compliment of hypocrisy; and the pillars of the republic that we thought so strong already bend under an increasing strain.

We honor Liberty in name and in form. We set up her statues and sound her praises. But we have not fully trusted her. And with our growth so grow her demands. She will have no half service!

Liberty! it is a word to conjure with, not to vex the ear in empty boastings. For Liberty means Justice, and Justice is the natural law—the law of health and symmetry and strength, of fraternity and co-operation.

They who look upon Liberty as having accomplished her mission when she has abolished hereditary privileges and given men the ballot, who think of her as having no further relations to the everyday affairs of life, have not seen her real grandeur—to them the poets who have sung of her must seem rhapsodists, and her martyrs fools! As the sun is the lord of life, as well as of light; as his beams not merely pierce the clouds, but support all growth, supply all motion, and call forth from what would otherwise be a cold and inert mass all the infinite diversities of being and beauty, so is liberty to mankind. It is not for an abstraction that men have toiled and died; that in every age the witnesses of Liberty have stood forth, and the martyrs of Liberty have suffered.

We speak of Liberty as one thing, and of virtue, wealth, knowledge, invention, national strength and national independence as other things. But, of all these, Liberty is the source, the mother, the necessary condition. She is to virtue what light is to color; to wealth what sunshine is to grain; to knowledge what eyes are to sight. She is the genius of invention, the brawn of national strength, the spirit of national independence. Where Liberty rises, there virtue grows, wealth increases, knowledge expands, invention multiplies human powers, and in strength and spirit the freer nation rises among her neighbors as Saul amid his brethren —taller and fairer. Where Liberty sinks, there virtue fades, wealth diminishes, knowledge is forgotten, invention ceases, and empires once mighty in arms and arts become a helpless prey to freer barbarians!

Only in broken gleams and partial light has the sun of Liberty yet beamed among men, but all progress hath she called forth.

Liberty came to a race of slaves crouching under Egyptian whips, and led them forth from the House of Bondage. She hardened them in the desert and made of them a race of conquerors. The free spirit of the Mosaic law took their thinkers up to heights where they beheld the unity of God, and inspired their poets with strains that yet phrase the highest exaltations of thought. Liberty dawned on the Phœnician coast, and ships passed the Pillars of Hercules to plow the unknown sea. She shed a partial light on Greece, and marble grew to shapes of ideal beauty, words became the instruments of subtlest thought, and against the scanty militia of free cities the countless hosts of the Great King broke like surges against a rock. She cast her beams on the four-acre farms of Italian husbandmen, and born of her strength a power came forth that conquered the world. They glinted from shields of German warriors, and Augustus wept his legions. Out of the night that followed her eclipse, her slanting rays fell again on free cities, and a lost learning revived, modern civilization began, a new world was unveiled; and as

Liberty grew, so grew art, wealth, power, knowledge, and refinement. In the history of every nation we may read the same truth. It was the strength born of Magna Charta that won Crecy and Agincourt. It was the revival of Liberty from the despotism of the Tudors that glorified the Elizabethan age. It was the spirit that brought a crowned tyrant to the block that planted here the seed of a mighty tree. It was the energy of ancient freedom that, the moment it had gained unity, made Spain the mightiest power of the world, only to fall to the lowest depth of weakness when tyranny succeeded liberty. See, in France, all intellectual vigor dying under the tyranny of the Seventeenth Century to revive in splendor as Liberty awoke in the Eighteenth, and on the enfranchisement of French peasants in the Great Revolution, basing the wonderful strength that has in our time defied defeat.

Shall we not trust her?

In our time, as in times before, creep on the insidious forces that, producing inequality, destroy Liberty. On the horizon the clouds begin to lower. Liberty calls to us again. We must follow her further; we must trust her fully. Either we must wholly accept her or she will not stay. It is not enough that men should vote; it is not enough that they should be theoretically equal before the law. They must have liberty to avail themselves of the opportunities and means of life; they must stand on equal terms with reference to the bounty of nature. Either this, or Liberty withdraws her light! Either this, or darkness comes on, and the very forces that progress has evolved turn to powers that work destruction. This is the universal law. This is the lesson of the centuries. Unless its foundations be laid in justice the social structure cannot stand.

Our primary social adjustment is a denial of justice. In allowing one man to own the land on which and from which other men must live, we have made them his bondsmen in a degree which increases as material progress goes on. This is the subtile alchemy that in ways they do not realize is extracting from the masses in every civilized country the fruits of their weary toil; that is instituting a harder and more hopeless slavery in place of that which has been destroyed; that is bringing political despotism out of political freedom, and must soon transmute democratic institutions into anarchy.

It is this that turns the blessings of material progress into a curse. It is this that crowds human beings into noisome cellars and squalid tenement houses; that fills prisons and brothels; that goads men with want and consumes them with greed; that robs women of the grace and beauty of perfect womanhood; that takes from little children the joy and innocence of life's morning.

Civilization so based cannot continue. The eternal laws of the universe forbid it. Ruins of dead empires testify, and the witness that is in every soul answers, that it cannot be. It is something grander than Benevolence, something more august than Charity—it is Justice herself that demands of us to right this wrong. Justice that will not be denied; that cannot be put off— Justice that with the scales carries the sword. Shall we ward the stroke with liturgies and prayers? Shall we avert the decrees of immutable law by raising churches when hungry infants moan and weary mothers weep?

Though it may take the language of prayer, it is blasphemy that attributes to the inscrutable decrees of Providence the suffering and brutishness that come of poverty; that turns with folded hands to the All-Father and lays on Him the responsibility for the want and crime of our great cities. We degrade the Everlasting. We slander the Just One. A merciful man would have better ordered the world; a just man would crush with his foot such an ulcerous ant-hill! It is not the Almighty, but we who are responsible for the vice and misery that fester amid our civilization. The Creator showers upon us his gifts—more than enough for all. But like swine scrambling for food, we tread them in the mire—tread them in the mire, while we tear and rend each other!

In the very centers of our civilization to-day are want and suffering enough to make sick at heart whoever does not close his eyes and steel his nerves. Dare we turn to the Creator and ask Him to relieve it? Supposing the prayer were heard, and at the behest with which the universe sprang into being there should glow in the sun a greater power; new virtue fill the air; fresh vigor the soil; that for every blade of grass that now grows two should spring up, and the seed that now increases fifty-fold should increase a hundred-fold! Would poverty be abated or want relieved? Manifestly no! Whatever benefit would accrue would be but temporary. The new powers streaming through the material universe could be utilized only through land. And land, being private property, the classes that now monopolize the bounty of the Creator would monopolize all the new bounty. Land owners would alone be benefited. Rents would increase, but wages would still tend to the starvation point!

This is not merely a deduction of political economy; it is a fact of experience. We know it because we have seen it. Within our own times, under our very eyes, that Power which is above all, and in all, and through all; that Power of which the whole universe is but the manifestation; that Power which maketh all things, and without which is not anything made that is made, has increased the bounty which men may enjoy, as truly as though the fertility of nature had been increased. Into the mind of one came the thought that harnessed steam for the service of mankind. To the inner ear of another was whispered the secret that compels the lightning to bear a message round the globe. In every direction have the laws of matter been revealed; in every department of industry have arisen arms of iron and fingers of steel, whose effect upon the production of wealth has been precisely the same as an increase in the fertility of nature. What has been the result? Simply that land owners get all the gain. The wonderful discoveries and inventions of our century have neither increased wages nor lightened toil. The effect has simply been to make the few richer; the many more helpless!

Can it be that the gifts of the Creator may be thus misappropriated with impunity? Is it a light thing that labor should be robbed of its earnings while greed rolls in wealth—that the many should want while the few are surfeited? Turn to history, and on every page may be read the lesson that such wrong never goes unpunished; that the Nemesis that follows injustice never falters nor sleeps! Look around to-day. Can this state of things continue? May we even say, "After us the deluge!" Nay; the pillars of the state are trembling even now, and the very foundations of society begin to quiver with pent-up forces that glow underneath. The struggle that must either revivify, or convulse in ruin, is near at hand, if it be not already begun.

The fiat has gone forth! With steam and electricity, and the new powers born of progress, forces have entered the world that will either compel us to a higher plane or overwhelm us, as nation after nation, as civilization after civilization, have been overwhelmed before. It is the delusion which precedes destruction that sees in the popular unrest with which the civilized world is feverishly pulsing only the passing effect of ephemeral causes. Between democratic ideas and the aristocratic adjustments of society there is an irreconcilable conflict. Here in the United States, as there in Europe, it may be seen arising. We cannot go on permitting men to vote and forcing them to tramp. We cannot go on educating boys and girls in our public schools and then refusing them the right to earn an honest living. We cannot go on prating of the inalienable rights of man and then denying the inalienable right to the bounty of the Creator. Even now, in old bottles the new wine begins to ferment, and elemental forces gather for the strife!

But if, while there is yet time, we turn to Justice and obey her, if we trust Liberty and follow her, the dangers that now threaten must disappear, the forces that now menace will turn to agencies of elevation. Think of the powers now wasted; of the infinite fields of knowledge yet to be explored; of the possibilities of which the wondrous inventions of this century give us but a hint. With want destroyed; with greed changed to noble passions; with the fraternity that is born of equality taking the place of the jealousy and fear that now array men against each other; with mental power loosed by conditions that give to the humblest comfort and leisure; and who shall measure the heights to which our civilization may soar? Words fail the thought! It is the Golden Age of which poets have sung and high-raised seers have told in metaphor! It is the glorious vision which has always haunted man with gleams of fitful splendor. It is what he saw whose eyes at Patmos were closed in a trance. It is the culmination of Christianity—the City of God on earth, with its walls of jasper and its gates of pearl! It is the reign of the Prince of Peace!

THE PROBLEM
OF
INDIVIDUAL LIFE

Henry George

The days of the nations bear no trace
    Of all the sunshine so far foretold;
The cannon speaks in the teacher's place—
    The age is weary with work and gold,
And high hopes wither, and memories wane;
    On hearths and altars the fires are dead;
But that brave faith hath not lived in vain—
    And this is all that our watcher said.
                                —*Frances Brown.*

My task is done.

Yet the thought still mounts. The problems we have been considering lead into a problem higher and deeper still. Behind the problems of social life lies the problem of individual life. I have found it impossible to think of the one without thinking of the other, and so, I imagine, will it be with those who, reading this book, go with me in thought. For, as says Guizot, "when the history of civilization is completed, when there is nothing more to say as to our present existence, man inevitably asks himself whether all is exhausted, whether he has reached the end of all things?"

This problem I cannot now discuss. I speak of it only because the thought which, while writing this book, has come with inexpressible cheer to me, may also be of cheer to some who read it; for, whatever be its fate, it will be read by some who in their heart of hearts have taken the cross of a new crusade. This thought will come to them without my suggestion; but we are surer that we see a star when we know that others also see it.

The truth that I have tried to make clear will not find easy acceptance. If that could be, it would have been accepted long ago. If that could be, it would never have been obscured. But it will find friends—those who will toil for it; suffer for it; if need be, die for it. This is the power of Truth.

Will it at length prevail? Ultimately, yes. But in our own times, or in times of which any memory of us remains, who shall say?

For the man who, seeing the want and misery, the ignorance and brutishness caused by unjust social institutions, sets himself, in so far as he has strength, to right them, there is disappointment and bitterness. So it has been of old time. So is it even now. But the bitterest thought—and it sometimes comes to the best and bravest—is that of the hopelessness of the effort, the futility of the sacrifice. To how few of those who sow the seed is it given to see it grow, or even with certainty to know that it will grow.

Let us not disguise it. Over and over again has the standard of Truth and Justice been raised in this world. Over and over again has it been trampled down—oftentimes in blood. If they are weak forces that are opposed to Truth, how should Error so long prevail? If Justice has but to raise her head to have Injustice flee before her, how should the wail of the oppressed so long go up?

But for those who see Truth and would follow her; for those who recognize Justice and would stand for her, success is not the only thing. Success! Why, Falsehood has often that to give; and Injustice often has that to give. Must not Truth and Justice have something to give that is their own by proper right—theirs in essence, and not by accident?

That they have, and that here and now, every one who has felt their exaltation knows. But sometimes the clouds sweep down. It is sad, sad reading, the lives of the men who would have done something for their fellows. To Socrates they gave the hemlock; Gracchus they killed with sticks and stones; and One, greatest and purest of all, they crucified. These seem but types. To-day Russian prisons are full, and in long processions, men and women, who, but for high-minded patriotism, might have lived in ease and luxury, move in chains towards the death-in-life of Siberia. And in penury and want, in neglect and contempt, destitute even of the sympathy that would have been so sweet, how many in every country have closed their eyes? This we see.

But do we see it all?

In writing I have picked up a newspaper. In it is a short account, evidently translated from a semi-official report, of the execution of three Nihilists at Kieff—the Prussian subject Brandtner, the unknown man calling himself Antonoff, and the nobleman Ossinsky. At the foot of the gallows they were permitted to kiss one another. "Then the hangman cut the rope, the surgeons pronounced the victims dead, the bodies were buried at the foot of the scaffold, and the Nihilists were given up to eternal oblivion." Thus says the account. I do not believe it. No; not to oblivion!

I have in this inquiry followed the course of my own thought. When, in mind, I set out on it I had no theory to support, no conclusions to prove. Only, when I first realized the squalid misery of a great city, it appalled and tormented me, and would not let me rest, for thinking of what caused it and how it could be cured.

But out of this inquiry has come to me something I did not think to find, and a faith that was dead revives.

The yearning for a further life is natural and deep. It grows with intellectual growth, and perhaps none really feel it more than those who have begun to see how great is the universe and how infinite are the vistas which every advance in knowledge opens before us—vistas which would require nothing short of eternity to explore. But in the mental atmosphere of our times, to the great majority of men on whom mere creeds have lost their hold, it seems impossible to look on this yearning save as a vain and childish hope, arising from man's egotism, and for which there is not the slightest ground or warrant, but which, on the contrary, seems inconsistent with positive knowledge.

Now, when we come to analyze and trace up the ideas that thus destroy the hope of a future life, we shall find them, I think, to have their source, not in any revelations of physical science, but in certain teachings of political and social science which have deeply permeated thought in all directions. They have their root in the doctrines, that there is a tendency to the production of more human beings than can be provided for; that vice and misery are the result of natural laws, and the means by which advance goes on; and that human progress is by a slow race development. These doctrines, which have been generally accepted as approved truth, do what, except as scientific interpretations have been colored by them, the extensions of physical science do not do—they reduce the individual to insignificance; they destroy the idea that there can be in the ordering of the universe any regard for his existence, or any recognition of what we call moral qualities.

It is difficult to reconcile the idea of human immortality with the idea that nature wastes men by constantly bringing them into being where there is no room for them. It is impossible to reconcile the idea of an intelligent and beneficent Creator with the belief that the wretchedness and degradation which are the lot of such a large proportion of human kind result from his enactments; while the idea that man mentally and physically is the result of slow modifications perpetuated by heredity, irresistibly suggests the idea that it is the race life, not the individual life, which is the object of human existence. Thus has vanished with many of us, and is still vanishing with more of us, that belief which in the battles and ills of life affords the strongest support and deepest consolation.

Now, in the inquiry through which we have passed, we have met these doctrines and seen their fallacy. We have seen that population does not tend to outrun subsistence; we have seen that the waste of human powers and the prodigality of human suffering do not spring from natural laws, but from the ignorance and selfishness of men in refusing to conform to natural laws. We have seen that human progress is not by altering the nature of men; but that, on the contrary, the nature of men seems, generally speaking, always the same.

Thus the nightmare which is banishing from the modern world the belief in a future life is destroyed. Not that all difficulties are removed—for turn which way we may, we come to what we cannot comprehend; but that difficulties are removed which seem conclusive and insuperable. And, thus, hope springs up.

But this is not all.

Political Economy has been called the dismal science, and as currently taught, *is* hopeless and despairing. But this, as we have seen, is solely because she has been degraded and shackled; her truths dislocated; her harmonies ignored; the word she would utter gagged in her mouth, and her protest against wrong turned into an indorsement of injustice. Freed, as I have tried to free her—in her own proper symmetry, Political Economy is radiant with hope.

For properly understood, the laws which govern the production and distribution of wealth show that the want and injustice of the present social state are not necessary; but that, on the contrary, a social state is possible in which poverty would be unknown, and all the better qualities and higher powers of human nature would have opportunity for full development.

And, further than this, when we see that social development is governed neither by a Special Providence nor by a merciless fate, but by law, at once unchangeable and beneficent; when we see that human will is the great factor, and that taking men in the aggregate, their condition is as they make it; when we see that economic law and moral law are essentially one, and that the truth which the intellect grasps after toilsome effort is but that which the moral sense reaches by a quick intuition, a flood of light breaks in upon the problem of individual life. These countless millions like ourselves, who on this earth of ours have passed and still are passing, with their joys and sorrows, their toil and their striving, their aspirations and their fears, their strong perceptions of things deeper than sense, their common feelings which form the basis even of the most divergent creeds—their little lives do not seem so much like meaningless waste.

The great fact which Science in all her branches shows is the universality of law. Wherever he can trace it, whether in the fall of an apple or in the revolution of binary suns, the astronomer sees the working of the same law, which operates in the minutest divisions in which we may distinguish space, as it does in the immeasurable distances with which his science deals. Out of that which lies beyond his telescope comes a moving body and again it disappears. So far as he can trace its course the law is ignored. Does he say that this is an exception? On the contrary, he says that this is merely a part of its orbit that he has seen; that beyond the reach of his telescope the law holds good. He makes his calculations, and after centuries they are proved.

Now, if we trace out the laws which govern human life in society, we find that in the largest as in the smallest community, they are the same. We find that what seem at first sight like divergences and exceptions are but manifestations of the same principles. And we find that everywhere we can trace it, the social law runs into and conforms with the moral law; that in the life of a community, justice infallibly brings its reward and injustice its punishment. But this we cannot see in individual life. If we look merely at individual life we cannot see that the laws of the universe have the slightest relation to good or bad, to right or wrong, to just or unjust.* Shall we then say that the law which is manifest in social life is not true of individual life? It is not scientific to say so. We would not say so in reference to anything else. Shall we not rather say this simply proves that we do not see the whole of individual life?

The laws which Political Economy discovers, like the facts and relations of physical nature, harmonize with what seems to be the law of mental development—not a necessary and involuntary progress, but a progress in which the human will is an initiatory force. But in life, as we are cognizant of it, mental development can go but a little way. The mind hardly begins to awake ere the bodily powers decline—it but becomes dimly conscious of the vast fields before it, but begins to learn and use its strength, to recognize relations and extend

---

* Let us not delude our children. If for no other reason than for that which Plato gives, that when they come to discard that which we told them as pious fable they will also discard that which we told them as truth. The virtues which relate to self do generally bring their reward. Either a merchant or a thief will be more successful if he be sober, prudent, and faithful to his promises; but as to the virtues which do not relate to self—

> "It seems a story from the world of spirits,
> When any one obtains that which he merits,
> Or any merits that which he obtains."

its sympathies, when, with the death of the body, it passes away. Unless there is something more, there seems here a break, a failure. Whether it be a Humboldt or a Herschel, a Moses who looks from Pisgah, a Joshua who leads the host, or one of those sweet and patient souls who in narrow circles live radiant lives, there seems, if mind and character here developed can go no further, a purposelessness inconsistent with what we can see of the linked sequence of the universe.

By a fundamental law of our minds—the law, in fact, upon which Political Economy relies in all her deductions—we cannot conceive of a means without an end; a contrivance without an object. Now, to all nature, so far as we come in contact with it in this world, the support and employment of the intelligence that is in man furnishes such an end and object. But unless man himself may rise to or bring forth something higher, his existence is unintelligible. So strong is this metaphysical necessity that those who deny to the individual anything more than this life are compelled to transfer the idea of perfectibility to the race. But as we have seen, and the argument could have been made much more complete, there is nothing whatever to show any essential race improvement. Human progress is not the improvement of human nature. The advances in which civilization consists are not secured in the constitution of man, but in the constitution of society. They are thus not fixed and permanent, but may at any time be lost—nay, are constantly tending to be lost. And further than this, if human life does not continue beyond what we see of it here, then we are confronted, with regard to the race, with the same difficulty as with the individual! For it is as certain that the race must die as it is that the individual must die. We know that there have been geologic conditions under which human life was impossible on this earth. We know that they must return again. Even now, as the earth circles on her appointed orbit, the northern ice cap slowly thickens, and the time gradually approaches, when its glaciers will flow again, and austral seas, sweeping northward, bury the seats of present civilization under ocean wastes, as it may be they now bury what was once as high a civilization as our own. And beyond these periods, science discerns a dead earth, an exhausted sun—a time when, clashing together, the solar system shall resolve itself into a gaseous form, again to begin immeasurable mutations.

What then is the meaning of life—of life absolutely and inevitably bounded by death? To me it seems intelligible only as the avenue and vestibule to another life. And its facts seem explainable only upon a theory which cannot be expressed but in myth and symbol, and which, everywhere and at all times, the myths and symbols in which men have tried to portray their deepest perceptions do in some form express.

The scriptures of the men who have been and gone—the Bibles, the Zend Avestas, the Vedas, the Dhammapadas, and the Korans; the esoteric doctrines of old philosophies, the inner meaning of grotesque religions, the dogmatic constitutions of Ecumenical Councils, the preachings of Foxes, and Wesleys, and Savonarolas, the traditions of red Indians, and beliefs of black savages, have a heart and core in which they agree—a something which seems like the variously distorted apprehensions of a primary truth. And out of the chain of thought we have been following there seems vaguely to rise a glimpse of what they vaguely saw—a shadowy gleam of ultimate relations, the endeavor to express which inevitably falls into type and allegory. A garden in which are set the trees of good and evil. A vineyard in which there is the Master's work to do. A passage—from life behind to life beyond. A trial and a struggle, of which we cannot see the end.

Look around to-day.

Lo! here, now, in our civilized society, the old allegories yet have a meaning, the old myths are still true. Into the Valley of the Shadow of Death yet often leads the path of duty, through the streets of Vanity Fair walk Christian and Faithful, and on Greatheart's armor ring the clanging blows. Ormuzd still fights with Ahriman—the Prince of Light with the Powers of Darkness. He who will hear, to him the clarions of the battle call.

How they call, and call, and call, till the heart swells that hears them! Strong soul and high endeavor, the world needs them now. Beauty still lies imprisoned, and iron wheels go over the good and true and beautiful that might spring from human lives.

And they who fight with Ormuzd, though they may not know each other—somewhere, sometime, will the muster roll be called.

Though Truth and Right seem often overborne, we may not see it all. How can we see it all? All that is passing, even here, we cannot tell. The vibrations of matter which give the sensations of light and color become to us indistinguishable when they pass a certain point. It is only within a like range that we have cognizance of sounds. Even animals have senses which we have not. And, here? Compared with the solar system our earth is but an indistinguishable speck; and the solar system itself shrivels into nothingness when gauged with the star depths. Shall we say that what passes from *our* sight passes into oblivion? No; not into oblivion. Far, far beyond our ken the eternal laws must hold their sway.

The hope that rises is the heart of all religions! The

poets have sung it, the seers have told it, and in its deepest pulses the heart of man throbs responsive to its truth. This, that Plutarch said, is what in all times and in all tongues has been said by the pure hearted and strong sighted, who, standing as it were, on the mountain tops of thought and looking over the shadowy ocean, have beheld the loom of land:

"Men's souls, encompassed here with bodies and passions, have no communication with God, except what they can reach to in conception only, by means of philosophy, as by a kind of an obscure dream. But when they are loosed from the body, and removed into the unseen, invisible, impassable, and pure region, this God is then their leader and king; they there, as it were, hanging on him wholly, and beholding without weariness and passionately affecting that beauty which cannot be expressed or uttered by men."

THE FUTURE
OF THE
HUMAN RACE
and
THE RELIGION
OF
REASON AND LOVE

[William] Winwood Reade

If we compare the present with the past, if we trace
events at all epochs to their causes, if we examine the
elements of human growth, we find that Nature has
raised us to what we are, not by fixed laws, but by provisional expedients ; and that the principle which in
one age effected the advancement of a nation, in the
next age retarded the mental movement, or even destroyed it altogether. War, despotism, slavery, and superstition, are now injurious to the progress of Europe,
but they were once the agents by which progress was
produced. By means of *War* the animated life was
slowly raised upward in the scale and quadrupeds passed
into man. By means of war the human intelligence
was brightened, and the affections were made intense ;
weapons and tools were invented ; foreign wives were
captured, and the marriages of blood relatives were for-
bidden ; prisoners were tamed, and the women set free ;
prisoners were exchanged, accompanied with presents ;
thus commerce was established, and thus, by means of
war, men were first brought into amicable relations with
one another. By war the tribes were dispersed all over
the world, and adopted various pursuits, according to the
conditions by which they were surrounded. By war the
tribes were compressed into the nation. It was war which
founded the Chinese Empire. It was war which unlocked
Babylonia, and Egypt, and India. It was war which developed the genius of Greece. It was war which planted
the Greek language in Asia, and so rendered possible the
spread of Christianity. It was war which united the world
in peace from the Cheviot Hills to the Danube and the
Euphrates. It was war which saved Europe from the
quietude of China. It was war which made Mecca the
center of the East. It was war which united the barons
in the crusades, and which destroyed the feudal system

Even in recent times the action of war has been useful in condensing scattered elements of nationality, and in liberating subject populations. United Italy was formed, directly or indirectly, by the wars of '59, '66, and '70. The last war realized the dreams of German poets, and united the Teutonic nations more closely than the shrewdest statesmen could have conceived to be possible a few years ago. That same war, so calamitous for France, will yet regenerate that great country, and make her more prosperous than she has ever been. The American War emancipated four million men, and decided for ever the question as to whether the Union was a nationality or a league. But the Crimean War was injurious to civilization; it retarded a useful and inevitable event. Turkey will some day be covered with corn-fields; Constantinople will some day be a manufacturing town; but a generation has been lost. Statesmen and journalists will learn, in time, that whatever is conquered for civilization is conquered for all. To preserve the balance of power was an excellent policy in the Middle Ages, when war was the only pursuit of a gentleman, and when conquest was the only ambition of kings. It is now suited only to the Highlands of Abyssinia. The jealousy with which true Britons regard the Russian success in Central Asia is surely a very miserable feeling. That a vast region of the earth should be opened, that robbery and rapine and slave-making raids should be suppressed, that waste-lands should be cultivated, that new stores of wealth should be discovered, that new markets should be established for the products of European industry—our own among the rest—that Russia should adjoin England in Asia as she adjoins Germany in Europe, what a lamentable occurrence, what an ominous event! In Central Africa

it often happens that between two barbarous and dis-
trustful nations there is a wide neutral ground, inhabited
by wild beasts, which prey upon the flocks and herds
on either side. Such is the policy which maintains the
existence of barbarous kingdoms between two civilized
frontiers. The great Turkish and Chinese Empires, the
lands of Morocco, Abyssinia, and Thibet, will be event-
ually filled with free, industrious, and educated populations. But those people will never begin to advance
until their property is rendered secure, until they enjoy
the rights of man; and these they will never obtain
except by means of European conquest. In British
India the peasant reaps the rice which he has sown;
and the merchant has no need to hide his gold beneath
the ground. The young men of the new generation are
looking forward to the time when the civil appoint-
ments of their country will be held by them. The Indian Mutiny was a mutiny only, and not a rebellion;
the industrious and mercantile classes were on the
English side. There is a sickly school of politicians
who declare that all countries belong to their inhabitants, and that to take them is a crime. If any country
in Asia did belong to its inhabitants, there might be
some force in this objection. But Asia is possessed
by a few kings and by their soldiers; these rulers are
usually foreigners; the masses of the people are inva-
riably slaves. The conquest of Asia by European
powers is therefore in reality emancipation, and is the
first step toward the establishment of Oriental nationality. It is needless to say that Europe will never engage in crusades to liberate servile populations; but
the pride and ignorance of military despots will provoke foreign wars, which will prove fatal to their rule.
Thus war will, for long years yet to come, be required

to prepare the way for freedom and progress in the East; and in Europe itself it is not probable that war will ever absolutely cease until science discovers some destroying force, so simple in its administration, so horrible in its effects, that all art, all gallantry, will be at an end, and battles will be massacres which the feelings of mankind will be unable to endure.

A second expedient of Nature is *Religion.* Men believe in the existence of beings who can punish and reward them in this life or in the next, who are the true rulers of the world, and who have deputed certain men, called priests, to collect tribute and to pass laws on their behalf. By means of these erroneous ideas, a system of government is formed to which kings themselves are subjected; the moral nature of man is improved, the sciences and arts are developed, distinct and hostile races are united. But error, like war, is only provisional. In Europe, religion no longer exists as a political power, but it will probably yet render service to civilization in assisting to Europeanize the barbarous nations whom events will in time bring under our control.

A third expedient of Nature is *the inequality of conditions.* Sloth is the natural state of man; prolonged and monotonous labor is hard for him to bear. The savage can follow a trail through the forest, or can lie in ambush for days at a time; this pertinacity and patience are native to his mind; they belong to the animals from whom he is descended; but the cultivation of the soil is a new kind of labor, and it is only followed from compulsion. It is probable that when domestic slavery was invented a great service was rendered to mankind; and it has already been shown that when prisoners of war were tamed and broken in, women were set free, and became beautiful, long-haired, low-voiced, sweet-eyed creatures, delicate in form, modest in demeanor, and refined in soul. It was also by means of slavery that a system of superfluous labor was established; for women, when slaves, are made only to labor for the essentials of life. It was by means of slavery that leisure was created, that the priests were enabled to make experiments and to cultivate the arts, that the great public buildings of the ancient lands were raised. It was slavery which arrested the progress of Greece ; but it was also slavery which enabled all the free men of a Greek town to be sculptors, poets, and philosophers. Slavery is now, happily, extinct, and can never be revived under the sanction of civilized authority. But a European Government ought perhaps to introduce compulsory labor among the barbarous races that acknowledge its sovereignty and occupy its land. Children are ruled and schooled by force, and it is not an empty metaphor to say that savages are children. If they were made to work, not for the benefit of others, but for their own ; if the rewards of their labor were bestowed, not on their masters, but on themselves —the habit of work would become with them a second nature, as it is with us, and they would learn to require luxuries which industry only could obtain. A man is not a slave in being compelled to work against his will, but in being compelled to work without hope and without reward. Enforced labor is undoubtedly a hardship, but it is one which at present belongs to the lot of man, and is indispensable to progress. Mankind grows because men desire to better themselves in life, and this desire proceeds from the inequality of conditions. A time will undoubtedly arrive when all men and women will be equal, and when the love of money, which is now the root of all industry, and which therefore is now the root of all good, will cease to animate the human mind. But changes so prodigious can only be effected in prodigious periods of time. Human nature cannot be transformed by a *coup d'état*, as the Communists imagine. It is a complete delusion to suppose that wealth can be equalized and happiness impartially distributed by any process of law, act of Parliament, or revolutionary measure. It is easy to compose a pathetic scene in a novel, or a loud article in a magazine, by contrasting Dives lunching on turtle at Birch's with Lazarus feeding on garbage in a cellar. But the poor man loses nothing because another man is rich. The Communist might as well denounce one man for enjoying excellent health while another man is a victim to consumption. Wealth, like health, is in the air; if a man makes a fortune, he draws money from Nature and gives it to the general stock. Every millionaire enriches the community. It is undoubtedly the duty of the Government to mitigate, so far as lies within its power, the miseries which result from over-population. But as long as men continue unequal in patience, industry, talent, and sobriety, so long there will be rich men and poor men—men who roll in their carriages, and men who die in the streets. If all the property of this country were divided, things would soon return to their original condition, unless some scheme could also be devised for changing human nature; and as for the system of the Commune, which makes it impossible for a man to rise or to fall, it is merely the old caste system revived; if it could be put into force, all industry would be disheartened, emulation would cease, mankind would go to sleep. It is not, however, strange that superficial writers should suppose that the evils of social life can be altered by changes in government and law. In the lands of the East, in the Spain and Portugal of the sixteenth century, in the France of the eighteenth century, in the American Colonies, and in England itself, whole classes were at one time plunged by misgovernment into suffering of body and apathy of mind. But a Government can confer few benefits upon a people except by destroying its own laws. The great reforms which followed the publication of the " Wealth of Nations " may all be summed up in the word Repeal. Commerce was regulated in former times by a number of paternal laws, which have since been, happily, withdrawn. The Government still pays with our money a number of gentleman to give us information respecting a future state, and still requires that in certain business transactions a document shall be drawn up with mysterious rites, in a mediæval jargon; but, placing aside hereditary evils, which, on account of vested interests, it is impossible at once to remove, it may fairly be asserted that the government of this country is as nearly perfect as any government can be. Power rests úpon public opinion, and is so beautifully poised that it can be overthrown and replaced without the business of the state being interrupted for a day. If the Executive is condemned by the nation, the press acts with irresistible force upon the Commons; a vote of censure is passed, and the rulers of a great empire abdicate their thrones. The House of Lords is also an admirable Upper Chamber; for if it were filled with ambitious men elected by the people it would enter into conflict with the Commons. And as for the Royal Image, it costs little and is useful as an emblem. The government of England possesses at the same time the freedom which is only found in a republic, and the loyalty which is only felt toward a monarch. Some writers believe that this monarchy is injurious to the public, and argue as follows: There are no paupers in America, and America is a republic. There are many paupers in England, and England is a monarchy. Therefore England should imitate America. It may astonish these writers to learn that America is in reality more of a monarchy than England. Buckingham Palace is a private dwelling; but the White House, though it has none of the pomp, has all the power, of a Court. The king of America has more to give away than any king of Great Britain since the time of Charles the Second. He has the power to discharge, at his own good pleasure and mere motion, every ambassador, every consul, every head of department, every government employé, down to the clerk on two hundred dollars a year, and to fill their places with his own friends. In America the opinion of the public can with difficulty act upon the Government. The press has no dignity, and very little power. Practices occur in the House of Representatives which have been unknown in England since the days of Walpole. If the prosperity of a country depended on its government, America would be less prosperous than England. But, in point of fact, America is the happiest country in the world. There is not a man in the vast land which lies between the oceans who, however humble his occupation may be, does not hope to make a fortune before he dies. The whole nation is possessed with the spirit which may be observed in Fleet Street and Cheapside: the boys sharp-eyed and curious, the men hastening eagerly along, even the women walking as if they had an object in view. There are in America no dull-eyed, heavy-footed

laborers, who slouch to and fro from their cottage to
their work, from their work to the beer-house, without
a higher hope in life than a sixpence from the squire
when they open a gate. There are no girls of the
milliner class who prefer being the mistresses of gentle-
men to marrying men of their own station with a Cock-
ney accent and red hands. The upper classes in
America have not that exquisite refinement which exists in the highest circles of society in Europe. But if
we take the whole people through and through, we find
them the most civilized nation on the earth. They
preserve in a degree hitherto without example the
dignity of human nature unimpaired. Their nobleness
of character results from prosperity; and their prosperity is due to the nature of their land. Those who
are unable to earn a living in the East have only to
move toward the West. This, then, is the reason that
the English race in America is more happy, more enlightened, and more thriving, than it is in the mother-
land. Politically speaking, the emigrant gains nothing;
he is as free in England as he is in America; but he
leaves a land where labor is depreciated, and goes to a
land where labor is in demand. That England may become as prosperous as America it must be placed under
American conditions; that is to say, food must be
cheap, labor must be dear, emigration must be easy. It
is not by universal suffrage, it is not by any act of
Parliament, that these conditions can be created. It
is Science alone which can Americanize England; it is
Science alone which can ameliorate the condition of
the human race.

When Man first wandered in the dark forest, he was
Nature's serf; he offered tribute and prayer to the
winds, and the lightning, and the rain; to the cave-lion,

which seized its burrow for its lair; to the mammoth, which devoured his scanty crops. But as time passed on, he ventured to rebel; he made stone his servant; he discovered fire and vegetable poison; he domesticated iron; he slew the wild beasts or subdued them; he made them feed him and give him clothes. He became a chief surrounded by his slaves; the fire lay beside him with dull red eye and yellow tongue waiting his instructions to prepare his dinner, or to make him poison, or to go with him to the war, and fly on the houses of the enemy, hissing, roaring, and consuming all. The trees of the forest were his flock, he slaughtered them at his convenience; the earth brought forth at his command. He struck iron upon wood or stone and hewed out the fancies of his brain; he plucked shells, and flowers, and the bright red berries, and twined them in his hair; he cut the pebble to a sparkling gem; he made the dull clay a transparent stone. The river, which once he had worshiped as a god, or which he had vainly attacked with sword and spear, he now conquered to his will. He made the winds grind his corn and carry him across the waters; he made the stars serve him as a guide. He obtained from salt and wood and sulphur a destroying force. He drew from fire and water the awful power which produces the volcano, and made it do the work of human hands. He made the sun paint his portraits, and gave the lightning a situation in the post-office.

Thus man has taken into his service, and modified to his use, the animals, the plants, the earths and the stones, the waters and the winds, and the more complex forces of heat, electricity, sunlight, magnetism, with chemical powers of many kinds. By means of his inventions and discoveries, by means of the arts and trades, and by means of the industry resulting **from** them, he has raised himself from the condition of **a serf** to the condition of a lord. His triumph, indeed, is incomplete ; his kingdom is not yet come. The Prince of Darkness is still triumphant in many regions of the world ; epidemics still rage, death is yet victorious. But the God of Light, the Spirit of Knowledge, the Divine Intellect, is gradually spreading over the planet and upward to the skies. The beautiful legend will yet come true : Ormuzd will vanquish Ahriman ; Satan will be overcome ; Virtue will descend from heaven, surrounded by her angels, and reign over the hearts of men. Earth, which is now a purgatory, will be made a paradise, not by idle prayers and supplications, but by the efforts of man himself, and by means of mental achievements analogous to those which have raised him to his present state. Those inventions and discoveries which have made him, by the grace of God, king of the animals, lord of the elements, and sovereign of steam and electricity, were all of them founded on experiment and observation. We can conquer Nature only by obeying her laws, and in order to obey her laws we must first learn what they are. When we have ascertained, by means of science, the method of Nature's operations, we shall be able to take her place and to perform them for ourselves. When we understand the laws which regulate the complex phenomena of life, we shall be able to predict the future, as we are already able to predict comets and eclipses and the planetary movements.

Three inventions, which perhaps may be long delayed, but which possibly are near at hand, will give to this overcrowded island the prosperous conditions of the United States. The first is the discovery of a motive force which will take the place of steam, with its cumbrous fuel of oil or coal; secondly, the invention of aerial locomotion which will transport labor at a trifling cost of money and of time to any part of the planet, and which, by annihilating distance, will speedily extinguish national distinctions; and thirdly, the manufacture of flesh and flour from the elements by a chemical process in the laboratory, similar to that which is now performed within the bodies of the animals and plants. Food will then be manufactured in unlimited quantities at a trifling expense; and our enlightened posterity will look back upon us who eat oxen and sheep just as we look back upon cannibals. Hunger and starvation will then be unknown, and the best part of the human life will no longer be wasted in the tedious process of cultivating the fields. Population will mightily increase, and the earth will be a garden. Governments will be conducted with the quietude and regularity of club committees. The interest which is now felt in politics will be transferred to science; the latest news from the laboratory of the chemist, or the observatory of the astronomer, or the experimenting room of the biologist, will be eagerly discussed. Poetry and the fine arts will take that place in the heart which religion now holds. Luxuries will be cheapened and made common to all; none will be rich, and none poor. Not only will man subdue the forces of evil that are without; he will also subdue those that are within. He will repress the base instincts and propensities which he has inherited from the animals below; he will obey the laws that are written on his heart; he will worship the divinity within him. As our conscience forbids us to commit actions which the conscience of the savage allows, so the moral sense of

our successors will stigmatize as crimes those offenses
against the intellect which are sanctioned by ourselves.
Idleness and stupidity will be regarded with abhor-
rence. Women will become the companions of men,
and the tutors of their children. The whole world will
be united by the same sentiment which united the
primeval clan, and which made its members think, feel,
and act as one. Men will look upon this star as their
fatherland; its progress will be their ambition; the
gratitude of others their reward. These bodies which
we now wear belong to the lower animals; our minds
have already outgrown them; already we look upon
them with contempt. A time will come when science
will transform them by means which we cannot con-
jecture, and which, even if explained to us, we could
not now understand, just as the savage cannot understand electricity, magnetism, steam. Disease will be
extirpated; the causes of decay will be removed; immortality will be invented. And then, the earth being
small, mankind will migrate into space, and will cross
the airless Saharas which separate planet from planet,
and sun from sun. The earth will become a Holy
Land which will be visited by pilgrims from all the
quarters of the universe. Finally, men will master the
forces of Nature; they will become themselves architects of systems, manufacturers of worlds. Man then
will be perfect; he will then be a Creator; he will
therefore be what the vulgar worship as a God. But
even then he will in reality be no nearer than he is at
present to the First Cause, the Inscrutable Mystery,
the GOD. There is but a difference in degree between
the chemist who to-day arranges forces in his laboratory so that they produce a gas, and the Creator who
arranges forces so that they produce a world; between

the gardener who plants a seed, and the Creator who plants a nebula. It is a question for us now to consider whether we have any personal relations toward the Supreme Power; whether there exists another world in which we shall be requited according to our actions. Not only is this a grand problem of philosophy; it is of all questions the most practical for us, the one in which our interests are most vitally concerned. This life is short, and its pleasures are poor; when we have obtained what we desire, it is nearly time to die. If it can be shown that, by living in a certain manner, eternal happiness may be obtained, then clearly no one except a fool or a madman would refuse to live in such a manner. We shall therefore examine the current theory respecting the nature of the Creator, the design of Creation, and the future destiny of Man. But before we proceed to this inquiry, we must first state that we intend to separate theology from morality. Whatever may be the nature of the Deity, and whether there be a future life or not, the great moral laws can be in no way changed. God is a purely scientific question. Whether he be personal or impersonal, definable or undefinable, our duties and responsibilities remain the same. The existence of a heaven and a hell can affect our calculations, but cannot affect our moral liabilities.

The popular theory is this: The world was made by a Great Being; he created man in his own image; and therefore his mind is analogous to that of man. But while our minds are imperfect, troubled by passions, stained with sin, and limited in power, his mind is perfect in beauty, perfect in power, perfect in love. He is omnipotent and omnipresent. He loves men whom he has made, but he sorrows over their transgressions. He has placed them on earth as a means of probation; those who have sinned and repent, those who are contrite and humble, he will forgive, and on them he will bestow everlasting happiness. Those who are wicked, and stubborn, and hard of heart, those who deny and resist his authority, he will punish according to his justice. This reward is bestowed, this punishment is inflicted, on the soul, a spirit which dwells within the body during life. It is something entirely distinct from the intellect or mind. The soul of the poorest creature in the streets and the soul of the greatest philosopher or poet are equal before the Creator; he is no respecter of person; souls are measured only by their sins. But the sins of the ignorant will be forgiven; the sins of the more enlightened will be more severely judged.

Now this appears a very reasonable theory as long as we do not examine it closely, and as long as we do not carry out its propositions to their full extent. But when we do so, we find that it conducts us to absurdity, as we shall very quickly prove.

The souls of idiots, not being responsible for their sins, will go to heaven; the souls of such men as Goethe and Rousseau are in danger of hell-fire. Therefore it is better to be born an idiot than to be born a Goethe or a Rousseau; and that is altogether absurd.

It is asserted that the doctrine of the immortality of the soul, and of happiness in a future state, gives us a solution of that distressing problem, the misery of the innocent on earth. But in reality it does nothing of the kind. It does not explain the origin of evil, and it does not justify the existence of evil. A poor helpless infant is thrust into the world by a higher force; it has done no one any harm, yet it is tortured in the most dreadful manner; it is nourished in vice, and crime, and disease; it is allowed to suffer a certain time and then it is murdered. It is all very well to say that afterward it was taken to everlasting bliss; but why was it not taken there direct? If a man has a child, and beats that child for no reason whatever, is it any palliation of the crime to say that he afterward gave it cake and wine?

This brings us to the character of the Creator. We must beg to observe again that we describe, not the actual Creator, but the popular idea of the Creator. It is said that the Supreme Power has a mind; this we deny, and to show that our reasons for denying it are good we shall proceed to criticise this imaginary mind.

In the first place, we shall state, as an incontrovertible maxim in morality, that a god has no right to create men except for their own good. This may appear to the reader an extraordinary statement; but had he lived in France at the time of Louis XIV., he would also have thought it an extraordinary statement that kings existed for the good of the people, and not people for the good of kings. When the Duke of Burgundy first propounded that axiom, St. Simon, by no means a servile courtier, and an enlightened man for his age, was " delighted with the benevolence of the saying, but startled by its novelty and terrified by its boldness." Our proposition may appear very strange, but it certainly cannot be refuted; for if it be said that the Creator is so great that he is placed above our laws of morality, then what is that but placing might above right? And if the maxim be admitted as correct, then how can the phenomena of life be justified?

It is said that the Creator is omnipotent, and also that he is benevolent. But one proposition contradicts the other. It is said that he is perfect in power, and that he is also perfect in purity. We shall show that he cannot possibly be both.

The conduct of a father toward his child appears to be cruel, but it is not cruel in reality. He beats the child, but he does it for the child's own good: he is not omnipotent; he is therefore obliged to choose between two evils. But the Creator is omnipotent; he therefore chooses cruelty as a means of education or development; he therefore has a preference for cruelty, or he would not choose it; he is therefore fond of cruelty, or he would not prefer it; he is therefore cruel, which is absurd.

Again, either sin entered the world against the will of the Creator, in which case he is not omnipotent, or it entered with his permission, in which case it is his agent, in which case he selects sin, in which case he has a preference for sin, in which case he is fond of sin, in which case he is sinful, which is an absurdity again.

The good in this world predominates over the bad; the good is ever increasing, the bad is ever diminishing. But if God is Love, why is there any bad at all? Is the world like a novel, in which the villains are put in to make it more dramatic, and in which virtue only triumphs in the third volume? It is certain that the feelings of the created have in no way been considered. If, indeed, there were a judgment-day, it would be for man to appear at the bar, not as a criminal, but as an accuser. What has he done that he should be subjected to a life of torture and temptation? God might have made us all happy, and he has made us all miserable. Is that benevolence? God might have made us all pure, and he has made us all sinful. Is that the perfection of morality? If I believed in the existence of this man-created God, of this divine Nebuchadnezzar, I would say, You can make me live in your world, O Creator, but you cannot make me admire it; you can load me with chains, but you cannot make me flatter you; you can send me to hell-fire, but you cannot obtain my esteem. And if you condemn me, you condemn yourself. If I have committed sins, you invented them, which is worse. If the watch you have made does not go well, whose fault is that? Is it rational to damn the wheels and the springs?

But it is when we open the Book of Nature, that book inscribed in blood and tears; it is when we study the laws regulating life, the laws productive of development—that we see plainly how illusive is this theory that God is Love. In all things there is cruel, profligate, and abandoned waste. Of all the animals that are born a few only can survive; and it is owing to this law that development takes place. The law of murder is the law of growth. Life is one long tragedy; creation is one great crime. And not only is there waste in animal and human life, there is also waste in moral life. The instinct of love is planted in the human breast, and that which to some is a solace is to others a torture. How many hearts yearning for affection are blighted in solitude and coldness. How many women seated by their lonely firesides are musing of the days that might have been. How many eyes when they meet these words which remind them of their sorrows will be filled with tears. Oh, cold, cruel, miserable life, how long are your pains. how brief are your delights! What are joys but pretty children that grow into regrets. What is happiness but a passing dream in

which we seem to be asleep, and which we know only
to have been when it is past.   Pain, grief, disease, and
death, are these the inventions of a loving God!   That
no animal shall rise to excellence except by being fatal
to the life of others, is this the law of a kind Creator!
It is useless to say that pain has its benevolence, that
massacre has its mercy.   Why is it so ordained that
bad should be the raw material of good?   Pain is not
less pain because it is useful; murder is not less murder because it is conducive to development.   *Here is
blood upon the hand still, and all the perfumes of Arabia
will not sweeten it.*

To this, then, we are brought with the much-
belauded theory of a semi-human Providence, an
anthropoid Deity, a Constructive Mind, and a Deus
Paleyensis, a God created in the image of a watch-
maker.   What, then, are we to infer?   Why, simply
this, that the current theory is false; that all attempts
to define the Creator bring us only to ridiculous
conclusions; that the Supreme Power is not a Mind, but
something higher than a Mind; not a Force, but something higher than a Force; not a Being, but something
higher than a Being; something for which we have no
words, something for which we have no ideas.   We
are to infer that Man is not made in the image of his
Maker, and that Man can no more understand his
Maker than the beetles and the worms can understand
him.   As men in the days of ignorance endeavored
to discover perpetual motion, and the philosopher's
stone, so now they endeavor to define God.   But in
time also they will learn that the nature of the Deity is
beyond the powers of the human intellect to solve.
The univérse is anonymous; it is published under
secondary laws; these at least we are able to investigate,

and in these perhaps we may find a partial solution of the great problem. The origin of evil cannot be explained, for we cannot explain the origin of matter. But a careful and unprejudiced study of Nature reveals an interesting fact and one that will be of value to mankind.

The Earth resembles a picture, of which we, like insects which crawl upon its surface, can form but a faint and incoherent idea. We see here and there a glorious flash of color; we have a dim conception that there is union in all its parts; yet to us, because we are so near, the tints appear to be blurred and confused. But let us expand our wings and flutter off into the air; let us fly some distance backward into Space until we have reached the right point of view. And now the colors blend and harmonize together, and we see that the picture represents *One Man.*

The body of a human individual is composed of cell-like bodies which are called "physiological units." Each cell or atom has its own individuality; it grows, it is nurtured, it brings forth young, and it dies. It is in fact an animalcule. It has its own body and its own mind. As the atoms are to the human unit, so the human units are to the human whole. There is only One Man upon the earth; what we call men are not individuals, but components; what we call death is merely the bursting of a cell; wars and epidemics are merely inflammatory phenomena incident to certain stages of growth. There is no such thing as a ghost or soul; the intellects of men resemble those instincts which inhabit the corpuscles, and which are dispersed when the corpuscle dies. Yet they are not lost; they are preserved within the body and enter other forms. Men therefore have no connection with Nature, except through

the organism to which they belong. Nature does not
recognize their individual existence. But each atom
is conscious of its life ; each atom can improve itself
in beauty and in strength ; each atom can, therefore,
in an infinitesimal degree, assist the development of the
Human Mind. If we take the life of a single atom,
that is to say, of a single man, or if we look only at a
single group, all appears to be cruelty and confusion ;
but when we survey mankind as One, we find it
becoming more and more noble, more and more divine,
slowly ripening toward perfection. We belong to the
minutiæ of Nature ; we are in her sight as the rain-
drop in the sky ; whether a man lives, or whether he
dies, is as much a matter of indifference to Nature as
whether a rain-drop falls upon the field and feeds a
blade of grass, or falls upon a stone and is dried to
death. She does not supervise these small details.
This discovery is by no means flattering, but it enlarges
our idea of the scheme of creation. That universe
must indeed be great in which human beings are so
small.

The following facts result from our investigations :
Supernatural Christianity is false. God-worship is
idolatry. Prayer is useless. The soul is not immortal.
There are no rewards and there are no punishments in
a future state.

It now remains to be considered whether it is right
to say so. It will doubtless be supposed that I shall
make use of the plea that a writer is always justified
in publishing the truth, or what he conscientiously
believes to be the truth, and that if it does harm he is
not to blame. But I shall at once acknowledge that
truth is only a means toward an end—the welfare of
the human race. If it can be shown that by speaking

the truth an injury is inflicted on mankind, then a stubborn adherence to truth becomes merely a Pharisee virtue, a spiritual pride. But, in moral life, Truth, though not infallible, is our safest guide, and those who maintain that it should be repressed must be prepared to bring forward irrefutable arguments in favor of their cause. If so much as the shadow of a doubt remains, their client, Falsehood, is non-suited, and Truth remains in possession of the conscience. Let us now hear what the special pleaders have to say. The advocates for Christianity *versus* Truth will speak first, and I shall reply; and then the advocates for deism will state their case. What they will endeavor to prove is this, that, even admitting the truth of my propositions, it is an immoral action to give them to the world. On the other hand, I undertake to show that the destruction of Christianity is essential to the interests of civilization; and also that man will never attain his full powers as a moral being until he has ceased to believe in a personal God and in the immortality of the soul.

" Christianity, we allow, is human in its origin, erroneous in its theories, delusive in its threats and its rewards. Jesus Christ was a man, with all the faults and imperfections of the prophetic character. The Bible is simply a collection of Jewish writings. The miracles in the Old Testament deserve no more attention from historians than the miracles in Homer. The miracles in the Gospels are like the miracles in Plutarch's Lives; they do not lessen the value of the biography, and the value of the biography does not lessen the absurdity of the miracles. So far we go with you. But we assert that this religion, with all its errors, has rendered inestimable services to civilization, and that it is so inseparably associated in the minds of men with purity of life and the precepts of morality, that it is impossible to attack Christianity without also attacking all that is good, all that is pure, all that is lovely in human nature. When you traveled in Africa did you not join in the sacrifices of the pagans? Did you not always speak with respect of their wood spirits and their water spirits, and their gods of the water and the sky? And did you not take off your shoes when you entered the mosque, and did you not, when they gave you the religious blessing, return the religious reply? And since you could be so tolerant to savages, surely you are bound to be more tolerant still to those who belong to your own race, to those who possess a nobler religion, and whose minds can be made by a careless word to suffer the most exquisite pain. Yet you attack Christianity, and you attack it in the wrong way. You ought, in the interests of your own cause, to write in such a manner that minds might be gradually trained to reflection, and decoyed to doubt. It is not only heartless and inhuman, it is also unwise, it is also unscientific, to say things which will shock and disgust those who are beginning to inquire, and it is bad taste to jest on subjects which, if not sacred in themselves, are held sacred in the eyes of many thoughtful and cultivated men. You ought to adopt a tone of reluctance, and to demonstrate against your will, as it were, the errors of the popular religion. Believers at least have a right to demand that if you discuss these questions upon which their hopes of eternal happiness are based, you will do so with gravity and decorum."

To this I reply that the religion of the Africans, whether pagan or moslem, is suited to their intellects, and is therefore a true religion; and the same may be said of Christianity among uneducated people. But Christianity is not in accordance with the cultivated mind; it can only be accepted or rather retained by suppressing doubts and by denouncing inquiry as sinful. It is therefore a superstition, and ought to be destroyed. With respect to the services which it once rendered to civilization, I cheerfully acknowledge them, but the same argument might once have been advanced in favor of the oracle at Delphi, without which there would have been no Greek culture, and therefore no Christianity. The question is not whether Christianity assisted the civilization of our ancestors, but whether it is now assisting our own. I am firmly persuaded that whatever is injurious to the intellect is also injurious to moral life; and on this conviction I base my conduct with respect to Christianity. That religion is pernicious to the intellect; it demands that the reason shall be sacrificed upon the altar; it orders civilized men to believe in the legends of a savage race. It places a hideous image, covered with dirt and blood, in the Holy of Holies; it rends the sacred Vail of Truth in twain. It teaches that the Creator of the Universe, that sublime, that inscrutable power, exhibited his back to Moses, and ordered Hosea to commit adultery, and Ezekiel to eat dung. There is no need to say anything more. Such a religion is blasphemous and foul. Let those admire it who are able. I, for my part, feel it my duty to set free from its chains as many as I can. Upon this point my conscience speaks clearly, and it shall be obeyed. With respect to manner and means, I shall use the arguments and the style best suited for my purpose. There has been enough of writing by implication and by inuendo; I do not believe in its utility, and I do not approve of its disguise. There should be no deceit in matters of religion. In my future assaults on Christianity I shall use the clearest language that I am able to command. Ridicule is a destructive instrument, and it is my intention to destroy. If a man is cutting down a tree, it is useless asking him not to strike so hard. But because I make use of ridicule, it does not follow that I am writing merely for amusement; and because I tear up a belief by the roots, it does not follow that I am indifferent to the pain which I inflict. Great revolutions cannot be accomplished without much anguish and some evil being caused. Did not the Roman women suffer when the Christians came and robbed them of their gods, and raised their minds, through pain and sorrow, to a higher faith? The religion which I teach is as high above Christianity as that religion was superior to the idolatry of Rome. And when the relative civilizations of the two ages are compared, this fetich of ink and paper, this Syrian book, is, in truth, not less an idol than those statues which obtained the adoration of the Italians and the Greeks. The statues were beautiful as statues; the book is admirable as a book; but the statues did not come down from heaven; the book was not a magical composition; it bears the marks not only of human genius, but also of human depravity and superstition.

As for the advocates of Deism, they acknowledge that Christianity is unsuited to the mental condition of the age; they acknowledge that the Bible ought to be attacked as Xenophanes attacked Homer; they acknowledge that the fables of a god impregnating a woman, of a god living on the earth, are relics of pagan superstition; they acknowledge that the doctrine of eternal punishment is incompatible with justice, and is there-

fore incompatible with God. But they declare that
Christianity should not be destroyed, but reformed;
that its barbarous elements should be expelled, and
that then, as a pure God-worship, it should be offered
to the world. "It is true that God is an idol, an image
made of human ideas which, to superior beings, would
appear as coarse and vile for such a purpose as the
wood and the stone of the savage appear to us. But
this idolatry is conducive to the morality of man. That
exquisite form which he raises in his mind, and before
which he prostrates himself in prayer, that God of
purity and love, becomes his ideal and example. As
the Greek women placed statues of Apollo and Narcis-
sus in their chambers that the beauty of the marble
form might enter their wombs through the windows of
their eyes, so by ever contemplating perfection the
mind is ennobled, and the actions born of it are divine.
And surely it is a sweet and consoling faith that there
is above us a great and benignant Being who, when the
sorrows of this life are past, will take us to himself.
How can it injure men to believe that the righteous
will be rewarded and that the wicked will be punished
in a future state? What good can be done by destroying a belief so full of solace for the sorrowful, so full of
promise for the virtuous, so full of terror for the workers of iniquity? You do not deny that 'much anguish
and some evil will be caused' by the destruction of
this belief; and what have you to show on the other
side? what will you place in the balance? Consider
what a dreadful thing it is to take even from a single
human being the hopes of a future life. All men cannot be philosophers; all cannot resign themselves with
fortitude and calm to the death-warrant of the soul.
Annihilation has perhaps more terrors for the mind

than eternal punishment itself. Oh, make not the
heart an orphan, cast it not naked and weeping on the
world. Take it not away from its Father, kill not its
hopes of an eternal home. There are mothers whose
children have gone before them to the grave, poor,
miserable women whose beauty is faded, who have
none to care for them on earth, whose only happiness
is in the hope that when their life is ended they will be
joined again to those whom they have lost. And will you
take that hope away? There are men who have passed
their whole lives in discipline and self-restraint, that
they may be rewarded in a future state. Will you tell
them that they have lived under an illusion, that they
would have done better to laugh, and to feast, and to
say, Let us make merry, for to-morrow we shall die?
There are men whom the fear of punishment in a
future life deters from vice and perhaps from crime.
Will you dare to spread a doctrine which unlooses all
restraints, and leaves men to the fury of their passions?
It is true that *we* are not demoralized by this belief in
the impersonality of God and the extinction of the
soul; but it would be a dangerous belief for those who
are exposed to strong temptations, and whose minds
have not been raised by culture to the religion of
dignity and self-control."

In the first place, I admit that the worship and contemplation of a man-like, but ideal, Being must have,
through the law of imitation, an ennobling effect on
the mind of the idolater, but only so long as the belief
in such a Being harmonizes with the intellect. It has
been shown that this theory of a benignant God is contradicted by the laws of Nature. We must judge of
the tree by its fruits; we must judge of the Maker by
that which he has made. The Author of the world

invented not only the good, but also the evil in the
world ; he invented cruelty ; he invented sin. If he
invented sin, how can he be otherwise than sinful ?
And if he invented cruelty, how can he be otherwise
than cruel ? From this inexorable logic we can only
escape by giving up the hypothesis of a personal
Creator. Those who believe in a God of Love must
close their eyes to the phenomena of life, or garble the
universe to suit their theory. This, it is needless to
say, is injurious to the intellect ; whatever is injurious
to the intellect is injurious to morality ; and, therefore,
the belief in a God of Love is injurious to morality.
God-worship must be classed with those provisional
expedients—Famine, War, Slavery, the Inequality of
Conditions, the Desire of Gain—which Nature em-
ploys for the development of man, and which she throws
aside when they have served her turn, as a carpenter
changes his tools at the various stages of his work.

The abolition of this ancient and elevated faith ;
the dethronement of God ; the extinction of piety as a
personal feeling ; the destruction of an image made of
golden thoughts in the exquisite form of an Ideal Man,
and tenderly enshrined in the human heart—these
appear to be evils, and such undoubtedly they are.
But the conduct of life is a choice of evils. We can
do nothing that is exclusively and absolutely good.
*Le genre humain n' est pas placé entre le bien et le mal,
mais entre le mal et le pire.* No useful inventions can be
introduced without some branch of industry being
killed and hundreds of worthy men being cast, without
an occupation, on the world. All mental revolutions
are attended by catastrophe. The mummeries and
massacres of the German Reformation, though known
only to scholars, were scarcely less horrible than those

of Paris in '93, and both periods illustrate the same
law.   I have facts in my possession which would enable
me to show that the abolition of the slave-trade, that
immortal and glorious event, caused the death of many
thousand slaves, who were therefore actually killed by
Sharp, Clarkson, Wilberforce, and their adherents.
But by means of abolition millions of lives have since
been saved.   The first generation suffered ; prisoners
were captured to be sold, and, the market having been
suppressed, were killed.   This was undoubtedly an
evil.   But then the slave-making wars came to an end,
and there was peace.   In the same manner I maintain
that even should the present generation be injured by
the abolition of existing faiths, yet abolition would be
justified.   Succeeding generations would breathe an
atmosphere of truth, instead of being reared in an
atmosphere of falsehood, and we who are so deeply
indebted to our ancestors have incurred obligations
toward our posterity.   Let us therefore purify the air,
and if the light kill a few sickly plants which have
become acclimatized to impurity and darkness, we
must console ourselves with the reflection that in
Nature it is always so, and that of two evils we have
chosen that which is the least.   But the dangers of the
truth are not so great as is commonly supposed.   It is
often said that if the fears of hell-fire were suddenly
removed, men would abandon themselves without restraint to their propensities and appetites ; recklessness
and despair would take possession of the human race,
and society would be dissolved.   But I believe that the
fears of hell-fire have scarcely any power upon earth at
all, and that when they do act upon the human mind it
is to make it pious, not to make it good.   A metaphysical theory cannot restrain the fury of the passions ; as

well attempt to bind a lion with a cobweb. Prevention of crime, it is well known, depends not on the severity, but on the certainty, of retribution. Just as a criminal is often acquitted by the jury because the penalties of the law are disproportioned to the magnitude of the offense, so the diabolical laws which inflict an eternal punishment for transitory sins have been tempered by a system of free pardons which deprives them of any efficiency they might have once possessed. What would be the use of laws against murder if the condemned criminal could obtain his liberty by apologizing to the Queen? Yet such is the Christian system, which, though in one sense beautiful on account of its mercy, is also immoral on account of its indulgence. The supposition that the terrors of hell-fire are essential or even conducive to good morals is contradicted by the facts of history. In the Dark Ages there was not a man or a woman, from Scotland to Naples, who doubted that sinners were sent to hell. The religion which they had was the same as ours, with this exception, that every one believed in it. The state of Europe in that pious epoch need not be described. Society is not maintained by the conjectures of theology, but by those moral sentiments, those gregarious virtues, which elevated men above the animals, which are now instinctive in our natures, and to which intellectual culture is propitious. For, as we become more and more enlightened, we perceive more and more clearly that it is with the whole human population as it was with the primeval clan: the welfare of every individual is dependent on the welfare of the community, and the welfare of the community depends on the welfare of every individual. Our conscience teaches us it is right, our reason teaches us it is

useful, that men should live according to the golden
rule.   This conduct of life is therefore enjoined
upon every man by his own instincts, and also by
the voice of popular opinion.   They cannot be happy
who are detested and despised by their fellow-men;
and as for those, the outlaws of society, who, like domestic animals run wild, herd together in secret places,
and, faithful only to their own gang, make war upon mankind, the Law, which is seldom evaded, the Law, which
never forgives, chases them from den to den, and makes
their lives as full of misery as they are full of crime.

The current religion is indirectly adverse to morals
because it is adverse to the freedom of the intellect.
But it is also directly adverse to morals by inventing
spurious and bastard virtues.   One fact must be familiar to all those who have any experience of human
nature.   A sincerely religious man is often an exceed-
ingly bad man.   Piety and vice frequently live together
in the same dwelling, occupying different chambers, but
remaining always on the most amicable terms.   Nor is
there anything remarkable in this.   Religion is merely
loyalty; it is just as irrational to expect a man to be
virtuous because he goes to church as it would be to
expect him to be virtuous because he went to court.
His king, it is true, forbids immorality and fraud.   But
the chief virtues required are of the lickspittle denomi-
nation—what is called a humble and a contrite heart.
When a Christian sins as a man, he makes compensa-
tion as a courtier.   When he has injured a fellow-
creature, he goes to church with more regularity, he
offers up more prayers, he reads a greater number of
chapters in the Bible, and so he believes that he has
cleared off the sins that are laid to his account.   This,
then, is the immorality of religion as it now exists.   It

creates artificial virtues and sets them off against actual vices. Children are taught to do this and that, not because it is good, but to please the king. When Christians are informed that not only our physical, but our moral, actions are governed by unchangeable law, and that the evil treatment of the mind, like the evil treatment of the body, is punished by a loss of happiness and health, they cry out against a doctrine which is so just and so severe. They are like the young Roman nobles who complained when the Tarquins were expelled, saying, that a king was a human being, that he could be angry and forgive, that there was room for favor and kindness, but that the law was a deaf and inexorable thing—*leges rem surdam inexorabilem esse*—that it allowed of no relaxation and indulgence—*nihil laxamenti nec veniæ habere*—and that it was a dangerous thing for weak and erring men to live by their integrity alone—*periculosum esse in tot humanis erroribus sola innocentia vivere.* Christians believe themselves to be the aristocracy of heaven upon earth; they are admitted to the spiritual court, while millions of men in foreign lands have never been presented. They bow their knees and say that they are miserable sinners, and their hearts rankle with abominable pride. Poor, infatuated fools! Their servility is real, and their insolence is real, but their king is a phantom and their palace is a dream.

Even with Christians of comparatively blameless lives their religion is injurious. It causes a waste of moral force. There are passionate desires of virtue, yearnings for the good, which descend from time to time like a holy spirit upon all cultivated minds, and from which, strange as it may seem, not even free-thinkers are excluded. When such an impulse animates the godless man, he expends it in the service of mankind; the

Christian wastes it on the air; he fasts, he watches, and
he prays. And what is the object of all his petitions and
salaams? He will tell you that he is trying to save his
soul. But the strangest feature in the case is this. He
not only thinks that it is prudent and wise on his part to
improve his prospects of happiness in a future state:
he considers it the noblest of all virtues. But there is
no great merit in taking care of one's own interests,
whether it be in this world or the next. The man who
leads a truly religious life in order to go to heaven is
not more to be admired than the man who leads a
regular and industrious life in order to make a fortune
in the city; and the man who endeavors to secure a
celestial inheritance by going to church, and by reading chapters in the Bible, and by having family
prayers, and by saying grace in falsetto with eyes
hypocritically closed, is not above the level of those
who fawn and flatter at Oriental courts in order to
obtain a monopoly or an appointment.

The old proverb holds good, in religious as in ordinary life, that self-preservation is the first law of Nature.
As long as men believe that there is a God or King who
will listen to their prayers and who will change his mind
at their request, as long as they believe that they can
obtain a mansion in the heavenly Belgravia, so long
they will place the duties of the courtier above the
duties of the man, so long they will believe that flattery
is pleasing to the Most High, so long they will believe
that they can offend against the law and escape the
penalties of the law, so long they will believe that acts
of devotion may be balanced against acts of immorality,
so long they will make selfishness a virtue, and salvation of the soul a higher principle of conduct than
social love. But when the faith in a personal God is

extinguished, when prayer and praise are no longer to be heard, when the belief is universal that with the body dies the soul, then the false morals of theology will no longer lead the human mind astray. Piety and virtue will become identical. The desire to do good, which arose in necessity, which was developed by the hopes of a heavenly reward, is now an instinct of the human race. Those hopes and illusions served as the scaffolding, and may now safely be removed. There will always be enthusiasts for virtue as there are now, men who adorn and purify their souls before the mirror of their consciences, and who strive to attain an ideal excellence in their actions and their thoughts. If from such men as these the hope of immortality is taken, will their natures be transformed? Will they who are almost angels turn straightway into beasts? Will the sober become drunkards? Will the chaste become sensual? Will the honest become fraudulent? Will the industrious become idle? Will the righteous love that which they have learned to loathe? Will they who have won by hard struggles the sober happiness of virtue return to the miseries of vice, by which few men have not at one time or another been enthralled? No; they will pass through some hours of affliction; they will bear another illusion to the grave; not the first that they have buried, not the first they have bewailed. And then, no longer able to hope for themselves, they will hope for the future of the human race, unable to believe in an eared God who listens to human supplications, they will coin the gold of their hearts into useful actions, instead of burning it as incense before an imaginary throne. We do not wish to extirpate religion from the life of man; we wish him to have a religion which will harmonize with his intellect, and which inquiry will strengthen, not destroy. We wish, in fact, to give him a religion, for now there are many who have none. We teach that there is a God, but not a God of the anthropoid variety, not a God who is gratified by compliments in prose and verse, and whose attributes can be catalogued by theologians. God is so great that he cannot be defined by us. God is so great that he does not deign to have personal relations with us human atoms that are called men. Those who desire to worship their Creator must worship him through Mankind. Such, it is plain, is the scheme of Nature. We are placed under secondary laws, and these we must obey. To develop to the utmost our genius and our love, that is the only true religion. To do that which deserves to be written, to write that which deserves to be read, to tend the sick, to comfort the sorrowful, to animate the weary, to keep the temple of the body pure, to cherish the divinity within us, to be faithful to the intellect, to educate those powers which have been entrusted to our charge and to employ them in the service of humanity—that is all that we can do. Then our elements shall be dispersed and all is at an end. All is at an end for the unit, all is at an end for the atom, all is at an end for the speck of flesh and blood with the little spark of instinct which it calls its mind; but all is not at an end for the actual Man, the true Being, the glorious One. We teach that the soul is immortal; we teach that there is a future life; we teach that there is a Heaven in the ages far away; but not for us single corpuscles, not for us dots of animated jelly, but for the One of whom we are the elements, and who, though we perish, never dies, but grows from period to period, and by the united efforts of single molecules called men, or of those cell-groups called nations, is raised toward the Divine power which he will finally attain. Our religion therefore is Virtue ; our Hope is placed in the happiness of our posterity ; our Faith is the Perfectibility of Man. A day will come when the European God of the nineteenth century will be classed with the gods of Olympus and the Nile ; when surplices and sacramental plate will be exhibited in the museums ; when nurses will relate to children the legends of the Christian mythology as they now tell them fairy tales. A day will come when the current belief in property after death (for is not existence property, and the dearest property of all ?) will be accounted a strange and selfish idea, just as we smile at the savage chief who believes that his gentility will be continued in the world beneath the ground, and that he will there be attended by his concubines and slaves. A day will come when mankind will be as the Family of the Forest, which lived faithfully within itself according to the golden rule in order that it might not die. But Love, not Fear, will unite the human race. The world will become a heavenly Commune to which men will bring the inmost treasures of their hearts, in which they will reserve for themselves not even a hope, not even the shadow of a joy, but will give up all for all mankind. With one faith, with one desire, they will labor together in the Sacred Cause—the extinction of disease, the extinction of sin, the perfection of genius, the perfection of love, the invention of immortality, the exploration of the infinite, the conquest of creation.

You blessed ones who shall inherit that future age of which we can only dream ; you pure and radiant beings who shall succeed us on the earth ; when you turn back your eyes on us poor savages, grubbing in the ground for our daily bread, eating flesh and blood, dwelling in vile bodies which degrade us every day to a level with the beasts, tortured by pains and by animal propensities, buried in gloomy superstitions, ignorant of Nature, which yet holds us in her bonds; when you read of us in books, when you think of what we are, and compare us with yourselves—remember that it is to us you owe the foundation of your happiness and grandeur, to us who now in our libraries and laboratories and star-towers and dissecting-rooms and workshops are preparing the materials of the human growth. And as for ourselves, if we are sometimes inclined to regret that our lot is cast in these unhappy days, let us remember how much more fortunate we are than those who lived before us, a few centuries ago. The working-man enjoys more luxuries to day than the King of England in the Anglo-Saxon times; and at his command are intellectual delights which but a little while ago the most learned in the land could not obtain. All this we owe to the labors of other men. Let us therefore remember them with gratitude; let us follow their glorious example by adding something new to the knowledge of mankind; let us pay to the future the debt which we owe to the past. All men indeed cannot be poets, inventors, or philanthropists; but all men can join in that gigantic and godlike work, the progress of creation. Whoever improves his own nature improves the universe of which he is a part. He who strives to subdue his evil passions—vile remnants of the old four-footed life—and who cultivates the social affections, he who endeavors to better his condition, and to make his children wiser and happier than himself, whatever may be his motives, he will not have lived in vain. But if he act thus not from mere prudence, not in the vain hope of being rewarded in another world, but from a pure sense of duty, as a citizen of Nature, as a patriot of the planet on which he dwells, then our philosophy, which once appeared to him so cold and cheerless, will become a religion of the heart, and will elevate him to the skies; the virtues, which were once for him mere abstract terms, will become endowed with life, and will hover round him like guardian angels, conversing with him in his solitude, consoling him in his afflictions, teaching him how to live and how to die. But this condition is not to be easily attained; as the saints and prophets were often forced to practice long vigils and fastings and prayers before their ecstacies would fall upon them and their visions would appear, so Virtue in its purest and most exalted form can only be acquired by means of severe and long-continued culture of the mind. Persons with feeble and untrained intellects may live according to their conscience, but the conscience itself will be defective. To cultivate the intellect is therefore a religious duty; and when this truth is fairly recognized by men, the religion which teaches that the intellect should be distrusted, and that it should be subservient to faith, will inevitably fall.

We have written much about inventions and discoveries and transformations of human nature, which cannot possibly take place for ages yet to come, because we think it good that the bright though distant future should be ever present in the eyes of man. But we shall now consider the existing generation, and we shall point out the work which must be accomplished, and in which all enlightened men should take a part. Christianity must be destroyed. The civilized world has outgrown that religion, and is now in the condition of the

Roman Empire in the pagan days. A cold-hearted infidelity above, a sordid superstition below; a school of Plutarchs who endeavor to reconcile the fables of a barbarous people with the facts of science and the lofty conceptions of philosophy; a multitude of augurs who sometimes smile when they meet, but who more often feel inclined to sigh, for they are mostly serious and worthy men. Entering the Church in their youth, before their minds were formed, they discover too late what it is that they adore, and since they cannot tell the truth, and let their wives and children starve, they are forced to lead a life which is a lie. What a state of society is this in which *free-thinker* is a term of abuse, and in which doubt is regarded as a sin. Men have a Bluebeard's chamber in their minds which they dare not open; they have a faith which they dare not examine, lest they should be forced to cast it from them in contempt. Worship is a conventionality, churches are bonnet shows, places of assignation, shabby-genteel *salons*, where the parochial At Home is given, and respectable tradesmen exhibit their daughters in the wooden stalls. O wondrous, awful, and divine Religion! You elevate our hearts from the cares of common life, you transport us into the unseen world, you bear us upward to that sublime temple of the skies where dwells the Vailed God, whom mortal eye can never view, whom mortal mind can never comprehend. How art thou fallen! How art thou degraded! But it will be only for a time. We are now in the dreary desert which separates two ages of belief. A new era is at hand.

It is incorrect to say, "theology is not a progressive science." The worship of ancestral ghosts, the worship of pagan deities, the worship of a single God, are suc-

cessive periods of progress in the science of Divinity.
And in the history of that science, as in the history of
all others, a curious fact may be observed. Those who
overthrow an established system are compelled to attack its founders, and to show that their method was
unsound, that their reasoning was fallacious, that their
experiments were incomplete. And yet the men who
create the revolution are made in the likeness of the
men whose doctrines they subvert. The system of
Ptolemy was supplanted by the system of Copernicus,
yet Copernicus was the Ptolemy of the sixteenth century. In the same manner, we who assail the Christian
faith are the true successors of the early Christians,
above whom we are raised by the progress of eighteen
hundred years.

As they preached against gods that were made of
stone, so we preach against gods that are made of ideas.
As they were called atheists and blasphemers, so are we.
And is our task more difficult than theirs? We have
not, it is true, the same stimulants to offer. We cannot
threaten that the world is about to be destroyed; we
cannot bribe our converts with a heaven, we cannot
make them tremble with a hell. But though our religion appears too pure, too unselfish, for mankind, it
is not really so, for we live in a noble and enlightened
age. At the time of the Romans and the Greeks, the
Christian faith was the highest to which the common
people could attain. A faith such as that of the Stoics
and the Sadducees could only be embraced by cultivated minds, and culture was then confined to a chosen
few. But now knowledge, freedom, and prosperity are
covering the earth; for three centuries past, human
virtue has been steadily increasing, and mankind is
prepared to receive a higher faith. But in order to

build we must first destroy. Not only the Syrian superstition must be attacked, but also the belief in a personal God, which engenders a slavish and Oriental condition of the mind; and a belief in a posthumous
reward, which engenders a selfish and solitary condition
of the heart. These beliefs are, therefore, injurious to
human nature. They lower its dignity; they arrest
its development; they isolate its affections. We shall
not deny that many beautiful sentiments are often min-
gled with the faith in a personal Deity, and with the
hopes of happiness in a future state; yet we maintain
that, however refined they may appear, they are selfish
at the core, and that if removed they will be replaced by
sentiments of a nobler and a purer kind. They cannot
be removed without some disturbance and distress; yet
the sorrows thus caused are salutary and sublime. The
supreme and mysterious Power by whom the universe
has been created, and by whom it has been appointed
to run its course under fixed and invariable law—that
awful One to whom it is profanity to pray, of whom it is
idle and irreverent to argue and debate, of whom we
should never presume to think, save with humility and
awe—that Unknown God has ordained that mankind
should be elevated by misfortune, and that happiness
should grow out of misery and pain. I give to universal
history a strange but true title—*The Martyrdom of Man.*
In each generation the human race has been tortured,
that their children might profit by their woes. Our
own prosperity is founded on the agonies of the past.
Is it therefore unjust that we also should suffer for the
benefit of those who are to come? Famine, pestilence,
and war are no longer essential to the advancement of
the human race. But a season of mental anguish is at
hand, and through this we must pass, in order that our

posterity may rise. The soul must be sacrificed; the hope in immortality must die. A sweet and charming illusion must be taken from the human race, as youth and beauty vanish never to return.

THE QUESTION OF BROTHERHOOD OR RELATEDNESS, AND OF THE REASONS FOR THE UNBROTHERLY, DIS-RELATED, OR UNPEACEFUL STATE OF THE WORLD, AND OF THE MEANS FOR THE RESTORATION OF RELATEDNESS

Nicholas Fyodorov

[NICHOLAS FYODOROV]

The Question of Brotherhood or Relatedness, and of the Reasons for the Unbrotherly, Dis-Related, or Unpeaceful State of the World, and of the Means for the Restoration of Relatedness

(A memorandum from the unlearned to the learned, both religious and secular, and to unbelievers as well as believers.) *

1.

In the disastrous year of 1891, when there was a famine—brought on by an apparently chronic drought—in many of the provinces which make up the granary of Russia, when rumors were constantly springing up which tended to increase the tense expectation of war, we suddenly heard about experiments in inducing rain by means of explosive substances which had hitherto been used exclusively, one might say, in foreign and domestic wars—revolutions, bomb-throwers' plots, etc. The coincidence of our famine from drought with the discovery of a means to combat drought, the very same means which had previously served only for mutual destruction, could not fail to produce a profound impression, particularly upon those who were close to the famine or who had close relatives in the age group which would have to enter the army's ranks in the event of war; and yet not only upon them! Man had in fact plainly done

---

* Translated for this volume by Ashleigh E. Moorhouse and George L. Kline from "*Vopros o bratstve, ili rodstve, o prichinakh nebratskovo, nerodstvennovo, t. e. nemirnovo, sostoyaniya mira, i o sredstvakh k vosstanovleniyu rodstva: Zapiska ot neuchonykh k uchonym, dukhovnym i svetskim, k veruyushchim i neveruyushchim,*" Pt. I, included in *Filosofiya obshchevo dela: Stati, mysli i pisma Nikolaya Fyodorovicha Fyodorova,* ed. V. A. Kozhevnikov and N. P. Peterson, Verny, 1906, I, 5-30. A few footnotes have been omitted, others have been shortened.

all the evil he could, both to nature (the exhaustion, despoiling, and plundering of it) and to his fellow man (the invention of the most deadly weapons and of the means of mutual destruction in general). . . .

And suddenly here, like a consoling ray of light for those "sitting in the darkness and shadow of death," came tidings which changed everything, the good tidings that the means invented for mutual destruction had become a means of salvation from famine, bringing the hope that now there would be an end to both famine and war, an end to war without the disarmament which is in fact impossible. . . .

Our hopes rest not on the possibility of producing rain by a few [cannon] shots or explosions, but on the possibility of controlling the moist and dry currents of air over broad areas, the possibility of saving men not only from drought but also from destructive downpours. This is a task which requires the common action of the armies of all nations, and therefore it must not under any circumstances become an object of mere [financial] speculation. The discovery of the possibility of producing rain by means of explosives, even if it did not justify the hopes which it has raised, would nevertheless not lose its significance as an indication of a method of action for the whole of the human race taken in its totality. . . .

At the present time everything serves war. There is not a single discovery which the military do not study with a view to its application to war; there is not a single invention which they have not tried to turn to the purposes of war. If armies were charged with the duty of adapting everything which they now adapt to war to the control of the forces of nature, the task of war would in fact be converted into the common task of the whole human race.

2.

The crop failure and especially the famine of 1891 compel the unlearned to remind the learned of their own origins, and of the obligation they are under as a result of these origins: (a) the obligation to turn to the study of the forces which produce crop failure and fatal plagues, i.e., to turn to a study of nature as a lethal force, devoting themselves to this study as a sacred duty, but also as a simple, natural, and reasonable one; and (b) the obligation to unite all men, the learned and the unlearned alike, in the task of studying and controlling this blind force. There can be no other obligation, no other task for a conscious being. To expect that the blind force which has been put under the control of this conscious being—but is not controlled by him—should of itself begin to produce only blessings and good harvests is utter childishness. . . .

Having divided up science and scholarship into a multitude of separate disciplines, the learned are saying that the oppressive calamities which have overtaken us fall within the purview of specialized disciplines and do not represent a general question for all men, i.e., the question of the dis-relatedness of this blind force with respect to rational human beings; this force obviously asks nothing of us but what it itself lacks, i.e., guiding reason, regulation. Of course such regulation is impossible as long as we are divided, but then there is division because there is no common task. It is the regulation or control of the forces of blind nature which constitutes the great task that can and must become common to all.

3.

The regulation of meteorological processes is necessary not just to guarantee a good harvest, not just for the sake of agriculture, but also in order to take the place of the forced underground labor of miners who dig for coal and iron, upon which the whole of modern industry is based. Regulation is necessary for the replacement of this digging by the extraction of energy directly from the currents of the atmosphere, from the energy of the sun which originally created the supply of coal, since the miners' position is so miserable that it would be unforgivable to forget them; it is precisely the enemies of society, the socialists, who are taking advantage of the miners' miserable position to stir up revolt. Thus the solution to both the agricultural and the industrial question lies in regulation and control of meteorological processes.

Practical reason, which is equal in scope to theoretical reason,

is controlling reason or regulation, i.e., the transformation of
the blind course of nature into one that is rational. Such a transformation is bound to appear to the learned as a disruption of
order, although this order of theirs brings only disorder among
men, striking them down with famine, plague, and death.

4.

The unlearned, bearing as they do all the consequences of dis-
relatedness, cannot avoid turning to the learned with the question of dis-relatedness, since the learned constitute the stratum
or class which, on the one hand, is an extreme expression of
dis-relatedness and, on the other, bears the obligation and has
the ability and opportunity of restoring relatedness—the class in
whose hands resides all knowledge and therefore also the solution to this question. However, they not only are not solving it
but, having created and supported the manufacturing industry
(the root of dis-relatedness) to satisfy an effeminate caprice, are
now inventing destructive weapons for the defense of this industry, once again motivated by effeminate caprice.

The unlearned are obligated to turn to the learned with the
question of dis-relatedness, and this obligation arises not simply
out of the present relationship of the learned to the unlearned,
but also out of the very origin of this former class. We would
be untrue to history if we explained the origin of the learned
as resulting from a temporary assignment or commission for
some purpose, just as the philosophers of the eighteenth century
were untrue to history when they explained the origin of the
state as due to an agreement or contract. There is of course no
juridical evidence of an assignment, but in history—understood in
moral categories—the emergence of the urban out of the rural
class, and of the learned out of the urban class must have the
significance of a temporary assignment. Otherwise this amounts
to a permanent disintegration, the complete negation of unity.

Thus while we may not be true to history in explaining the
origin of the learned class as the result of a temporary assignment, while we may not agree on how this really took place,
we are at least true to morality, i.e., to how things ought to
be. A truly moral being has no need for compulsion, command,

or force. He himself is aware of his obligation, revealing it in all its fullness. He himself issues an assignment to himself and indicates what must be done for those from whom he has been isolated, since the isolation (whether it be compulsory or voluntary) cannot be irrevocable. Indeed, it would be criminal to renounce those from whom one has sprung, to forget about their welfare.

Moreover, if the learned were to behave in this way it would mean that they would be renouncing their own welfare, too, that they would remain forever as prodigal sons, eternal hired servants, slaves of urban caprice, completely heedless of the needs of the rural population, which are the genuine needs, since the needs of those who are unspoiled by urban influences are limited to the daily necessities which offer security against famine and sickness, against those things which destroy not only life but also relatedness, substituting enmity and hostility for love. The rural question is, first, the question of the dis-relatedness among people who through ignorance have forgotten their relatedness; and second, the question of the dis-relatedness of nature to people, i.e., that dis-relatedness which is felt preeminently in the villages, standing as they do in direct relationship to this blind force. In the cities, which are remote from nature, one can only *imagine* that one lives a life that is one with the life of nature.

5.

The hostile dividedness of the world and all the misfortunes stemming from this also compel us—i.e., the unlearned, those who put work above thought (work that is common to all, and not simply strife)—to turn to the learned, and especially to the theologians . . . , to those who put thought above work, with this memorandum concerning dis-relatedness and the means of restoring relatedness. The separation of thought from work (both of which have become the property of special classes) is the greatest of all misfortunes, incomparably worse than the separation into rich and poor. Socialism and in general our whole age attach the greatest significance to the division into rich and poor, assuming of course that with the removal of this division the other will also disappear and everyone will become educated. But we are thinking not of popular education, which, with the elimination of poverty, will certainly be distributed more equally. We are thinking rather of an actual participation in the pursuit of knowledge, the common participation of all men, without which the division into learned and unlearned will not disappear. This cannot be brought about by the removal of poverty alone. So long as everyone does not participate in the pursuit of knowledge, pure science and scholarship will remain indifferent to conflict and destruction, and applied science will continue to further it, either directly by the invention of destructive weapons, or indirectly by lending a seductive appearance to objects of consumption, thus introducing hostility among men.

Science and scholarship, taking no direct personal part in conflict or war, and standing beyond the reach of natural misfortunes, shielded by the peasantry—who stand in an immediate relationship to nature—from these misfortunes, science remains indifferent to the exhaustion of natural energies and to the changes of weather which for townspeople may be rather pleasant, even though they produce a crop failure. Only when all people are participants in the pursuit of knowledge will pure science and scholarship (which now sees nature as a sphere in which the sentient is sacrificed to the insentient) cease being indifferent to such a perverted relationship between the sentient and the insentient. Applied science will cease to be the companion and ally of insentient forces and will convert weapons of destruction into instruments for the regulation of the blind death-dealing force of nature. . . .

The solution of the second problem—concerning the division into rich and poor—depends on the solution of the first—the problem of the division into learned and unlearned (men of thought and men of work). The problem of the division between men of thought and men of work has as its starting point such common misfortunes as sickness and death, and requires for its solution not wealth or luxury but a higher good, the participation of all in art and knowledge as applied to the solution of the problem of dis-relatedness and the restoration of relatedness—which means a quest for the Kingdom of God.

6.

In raising the question of "brotherhood and the reasons for the unbrotherly state of the world," we have in mind above all else the conditions under which brotherhood can and must be actualized, i.e., this is a practical question, a question in the sense that one speaks of an Eastern Question, a Question of Colonization, Emigration, etc. This is a question of what must be done to bring an end to the unbrotherly state. As such the question is obligatory for all sons of men and all the more so for those who have been baptized in the name of the God of all fathers. This is not a learned question, not a matter of research, even though it very much concerns the learned insofar as the question of knowledge, or science and scholarship (the theoretical question), is already a necessary, antecedent, and integral part of the practical question.

7.

By calling all that is involved in the title of this memorandum addressed by the unlearned to the learned a "question," by calling it all the raising of a question, we at once admit and wish to make clear our own weakness in comparison with those to whom we are addressing the question. Those who ask questions are not those who know the answers, but those who are conscious of their own weakness; and this is not an expression of the sort of modesty usually found in prefaces, but an inescapable humility in the face of the terrible power which causes non-brotherhood and thus forces us toward unity, compelling us to speak to those with whom we are not accustomed to speak. This is a humility before a power which causes all special interests to fall silent.

If Russia, or Russian science and scholarship, were to turn with this question to nations which stand above her intellectually and morally, there would be nothing in the question to offend the pride of such advanced nations.

8.

The unbrotherly state, of course, has its serious causes: we are all living in conditions which raise the question of non-brotherhood. Thus, in formulating this question we are not separating ourselves from the people but are expressing the common mind or spirit [*dukh*] of all. . . . Non-brotherhood is not rooted in caprice; it cannot be eradicated by words, and wishing alone is powerless to remove its causes. What is needed is the combined work of knowledge and action, since a stubborn sickness of this sort, having its roots both within and outside of man, is not to be healed in the wink of an eye, as those people think who are led only by feeling, whose statements about non-brotherhood may be called "treatises on the groundlessness of the unbrotherly state"; they forbid thought because thinking or reflection is a laying bare of reasons and conditions.

Belief in the groundlessness of the unbrotherly state leads not to real peace, to brotherhood, but only to playing at peace, to comedies of reconciliation which create a pseudo-peaceful state, a false peace that is much worse than open hostility, because the latter raises the question, while an imaginary reconciliation conceals and perpetuates enmity. Tolstoy preaches such a doctrine: having quarreled one day, he goes to make up the quarrel the next. Not only does he not take any steps to prevent clashes; he actually seems to seek them out, perhaps simply in order to conclude an unstable peace later on.

But causation, in the sense of determinism, can be admitted only for men taken in isolation, in division. The learned class accepts a fateful, eternal determinism precisely because it does not believe in combined action. The utter irremovability of the unbrotherly state is a fundamental dogma of the learned as a class, since an admission of the removability of the causes of the unbrotherly state by the combined effort of all people would require the transformation of the learned class into a commission or "task force."

9.

By "unbrotherly state" we mean all juridically fixed economic relations, social hierarchies, and international divisions. In speaking of the question of the causes of dis-relatedness we are using "dis-relatedness" to mean the "citizen-ship" or "civilization" which has replaced "brotherliness," we have in mind the "stateness" [*gosudarstvennost*] which has replaced "fatherland-ness" [*otechestvennost*]. Fatherland-ness is not the same as patriotism, which instead of loving one's forefathers makes them an object of one's pride, replacing love or virtue by pride and vice, love of one's forefathers by love of oneself, by self-love. People who are proud of the same thing may form an honorary society, but not a brotherhood of sons who love one another. However, as soon as pride in the exploits of one's forefathers is replaced by contrition for their death, as soon as the earth is seen as a cemetery and nature as a death-dealing force, just so soon will the political question be replaced by the physical question; and in this context the physical will not be separated from the astronomical, i.e., the earth will be recognized as a heavenly body and the stars will be recognized as other earths. The unification of all sciences under astronomy is the simplest, most natural, unlearned thing, required as much by the feelings as by the non-abstract intellect, since by such a unification mythical "patrolatry" is transformed into a real raising of the dead, into a regulation of all worlds by all the resurrected generations.

The question of the force which compels the two sexes to unite in one flesh as a transition to the being of a third by means of childbearing is the question of death: a man's exclusive adherence to his wife forces him to forget his forefathers and brings political and civil enmity into the world. At the same time it compels him to forget that the earth is a body located in space and that the heavenly bodies are earths. As long as historical life was only oceanic or coastal, as long as it embraced only a small part of the earth, with approximately the same conditions of life, it was a political, civil, or commercial history —a civilization, i.e., a struggle. But when the interiors of the continents enter into history, i.e., when the whole earth becomes historical, then the question of states and cultures will become a question of physics or astrophysics, a question of the earth as a heavenly body.

10.

By refusing to grant ourselves the right to set ourselves apart from the mass of people (the crowd), we are kept from setting any goal for ourselves that is not the common task of all, and so we cannot neglect the question of non-brotherhood. We did not raise it and we will not resolve it. We live constantly in conditions which provoke the question; it is as impossible not to think about it as it is to arrest the process of thought and reflection in one's head. There is only one doctrine which requires not separation but reunification, which has not artificial goals but a single, common, completely natural goal for all; this is the doctrine of relatedness. . . . Does this not point to the true goal of the human race? For it is not self-preservation but the restoration of life to our forefathers which must be our goal. The punishment of the confusion of tongues came precisely because the living generation wanted to raise a memorial to itself. . . .[1]

The question of the individual and the crowd is resolved only in the doctrine of relatedness. Unity does not engulf but rather exalts each unit, while the difference of individuals only strengthens the unity which includes them all first, in the awareness by each that he is a son, a grandson, a great-grandson, a descendant, i.e., a son of all his dead forefathers, and not a vagabond in a crowd having no sense of relatedness; and second, in the acknowledgment by each together with all others (not in diversity or separateness as in a crowd) of his duty toward them, toward all his dead forefathers, a duty the limitations of which proceed only from his sensuous nature or, more

1. "Life in and for another" (altruism) is the grossest distortion of the words of the Saviour "that they may be made one . . ." which speaks precisely about *all* men, while "life in and for another" can only refer to people taken in isolation. Christianity . . . is not altruism; it knows only *all* men. . . . Only a life "with all and for all" will be a fulfillment of the Son's prayer to his Father for all sons who are living and all fathers who have died. . . .

accurately, from the abuse of his sensuous nature, which 'is fragmenting the mass of people (the rural population) and·turning it into a crowd.

The mass of mankind will be transformed from a crowd, a jostling and struggling throng, into a harmonious power when the rural mass or common people [*narod*] become a union of sons for the resurrection of their fathers, when they become a relatedness, "a psychocracy." The transformation of the "crowd" into a union of sons who find their unity in their fathers' work is precisely a fusion as opposed to a confusion. In this task of all the fathers, taken as one father, each will become a great man, a participant in the greatness of the task; he becomes incomparably greater than any of those who have been called "great." Only a son of man is a great man, a man who has entered into the measure of the stature of Christ. No so-called "great man" has attained this stature. The conception of a son of man includes the whole race, while the task which gives him this name is the transformation of blind, death-dealing forces into forces that will restore life to all fathers. To attain to the measure of the stature of Christ means to become in fact a son of man, for Christ called Himself the Son of Man.

The humanist who calls himself a *"man,"* and is proud of this name, has clearly not yet come to the measure of the stature of Christ, has not yet become a *son of man*. And all those who in our time have rejected the cult of the fathers have thereby deprived themselves of the right to be called sons of man. Instead of taking part in the common task they have become mere organs or instruments of various enterprises, mere cogs and valves, even though they think they are living for themselves. Such a situation makes it possible to understand that neither the eternal existence of these "*x*'s and *y*'s" (as Noiré says: "No one would assert that the eternal existence of individual *x*'s and *y*'s has any exceptional significance") nor even their transitory existence can have any meaning, so that it would be better if they had not existed at all. But of course this is true only of *x*'s and *y*'s and cannot refer to the *sons of man, to those who restore life*, whose existence not only has an exceptional significance but also is absolutely inevitable if the goal of life is the transformation of the blind force of nature into a force controlled by the reason of all the resurrected generations. At that time, of course, *everyone*, down to the *last man*, will be necessary.

11.

The question which forms the subject of the present memorandum has a twofold significance:

1. When we compare the question of the causes of non-brotherhood to the Eastern Question, the Question of Emigration, etc., we mean that science must not be the knowledge of causes only without the knowledge of goals, must not be the knowledge of initiating causes only without the knowledge of final causes (i.e., must not be knowledge for the sake of knowledge, or knowledge without action); it must not be knowledge of *what is* without a knowledge of what *ought to be*. This means that science must be the knowledge not of causes *in general,* but precisely of the causes of non-brotherhood; it must be knowledge of the causes of the *division* which makes us instruments of the blind forces of nature, the displacing of the older generation by the younger, and the mutual crowding which leads to this displacement. Such is the general significance of the question of non-brotherhood. Hence it follows that the meaning of brotherhood is included in the unification of all men in the common task of transforming the blind forces of nature into an instrument of the reason of the whole human race for the restoration to life of those who have been displaced.

2. However, when those who acknowledge their ignorance (the unlearned) turn to the learned with the question of the causes of non-brotherhood, the question arises whether the learned should remain a class or school, whether the learned should refuse to answer this question, on the grounds that science is only an investigation of causes *in general (scholasticism),* or whether they, the learned, ought to turn themselves into a commission or task force for the elucidation and critical explication of the question of the causes of division. The question arises whether the learned ought to look upon their separation from the mass of mankind as only a temporary assignment, or as a final goal. Whether they ought

to see themselves simply as "scouts" along the road that lies ahead or whether they are the best and highest class, the blossom and fruit of the whole life of the human race. The question arises about the learned and the intelligentsia, about the inner discord of the intellect deprived of feeling and will, the question of complete dis-relatedness as the essential characteristic of the learned, inevitably stemming from the separation of the intellect from feeling and will.

An inner discord is concealed in the external discord, in the separation of the learned and intelligent classes from the people. Knowledge deprived of feeling will be knowledge only of causes in general, and not the study of the causes of dis-relatedness; the intellect separated from the will will be knowledge of evil without the effort to eradicate it, and knowledge of good without the desire to establish it; i.e., it will be the acceptance of dis-relatedness rather than a project for the restoration of relatedness. Dis-relatedness is a consequence of the lack of feeling, a forgetting of the fathers, a falling out of the sons. (In its causes dis-relatedness involves all of nature, as a blind force not controlled by reason.) But as soon as intellect arrives at feeling there is remembrance of the dead fathers (in museums), together with the union of the sons of these dead fathers and of the fathers who are still living (the religious community—[sobor]) for the education of their sons (the school). But the fullness of feeling is the union of all living men (the sons), while the fullness of will or combined action of all the living is the raising to life of all who are the dead (fathers), the religious community of all the living, the union of those who have been born for the resurrection of those who have been put to death as a result of childbearing and child-rearing. What is needed now so that the museum and the community may attain this fullness?

If the subject of science is the resolution of the question of causes in general, this means that science is occupied with the question, "Why does that which exists exist?" Both of these questions clearly mean the same thing. But the question, "Why does that which exists exist?" is obviously an unnatural, completely artificial question. How unnatural it is to ask, "Why *does that which exists exist?"* and yet how completely natural it is to ask, *"Why do the living die?"* Both this question and the question of brotherhood would be raised by the philosophers and scientists if brotherhood existed among men; but in the absence of brotherhood they do not see the question, or at least they do not turn it into a task or make it the goal of their studies. Yet this purpose is really the only one which can give meaning to the existence of philosophers and scientists, not as a class, but simply as a temporary commission or task force.

12.

. . . In exchanging their position as an upper class for that of a commission or task force, the learned will be losing only their imaginary superiority and will be acquiring a real superiority. The world will then be not a mere representation (which it inevitably is for closeted scholars deprived of activity and condemned to contemplation and wishful thinking, without the means of bringing anything about). The representation of the world will then become a project for a better world, and the organizing and actualization of this project will be the commission's task. Pessimism will disappear but will not give way to that optimism which only seduces, striving to represent the world as better than it is. There will be no point then in concealing evil from ourselves; there will be no point then in trying to convince ourselves that death does not exist. Instead, while acknowledging the existence of evil in all its power, we shall not lose the hope that in uniting all rational powers we will find a way to give direction to the irrational power which brings evil and death and all that follows from the latter.

By acknowledging an immanent raising of the dead, we set a limit to that human curiosity which is directed toward the transcendent, toward thought without work. And yet by condemning spiritualism and in general the striving toward what is other-worldly, we are not laying a restraint upon man, since we are showing that the sphere of that which is accessible and immanent is so broad that the moral sense of relatedness, or all-embracing love, will find complete satisfaction therein.

Three vices inevitably result from the separation of the learned into a special class: the first and fundamental one is the transformation of the world into an idea, a representation, or fiction. That which in life constitutes egoism, solipsism, and all the crimes stemming from them, has found its formula in the philosophical expression, "The world is my idea or representation" (egoism), which is indeed the final result of all critical [i.e., Kantian] philosophy. The transformation of the world into an idea or a representation is the last word of the learned class. Generated by idleness or external inactivity (if thinking is not to be regarded as work or activity) and individualism, the transformation of the world into an idea or representation is the last offspring of idleness, which is the mother of vice, or of solipsism (egoism), which is the father of crime. Two other vices result from this major vice (the transformation of the world into a representation): drug addiction and hypnosis. For if the world is an idea or representation, then the transformation of unpleasant ideas or representations into pleasant ones by means of drugs would solve the world problem since this would eliminate all suffering, replacing it by pleasure. Hypnosis solves the problem even more simply: it thinks that it can save people from all sickness and vice simply by the power of wishing. . . .

13.

Positivism, the last word of European thought, is not a departure from the schools and hence from the learned class. Positivism too is based on the separation of theoretical and practical reason. The impotence of theoretical reason is explained by its inaction, the absence of any unification in a common task. Positivism is only another form of metaphysical scholasticism which in itself, by way of a similar transformation, grew out of theological scholasticism. It too is a scholasticism, and positivists constitute a school rather than a commission in the sense explained above. However, if the positive movement were opposed not to what is metaphysical or theological but to what is popular [narodny] and religious (to what is not mere knowledge or contemplation but also action, sacrifice, cult, although only a mythical action, i.e., a miraculous, unreal, imaginary means against evil)—then the positive school would convert this mythical, miraculous, or fictitious action into a real and genuine means against evil. It would not remain an unsatisfied need which, as a result of ignorance of what is real, is satisfied with or rather is simply drowned in imaginary activity, in an imaginary means against evil.

If positivism (it makes no difference whether it is Western and European or Eastern and Oriental) were really to oppose everything mythical and fictitious, then there would be nothing arbitrary about it. But now positivism in fact prides itself on its limitations and denials; it does not replace the fictitious by the real but only negates the former. . . . Rejecting what is essential, positivism indulges man's artificial needs, needs which are satisfied, or rather stimulated, by industry. It is clear that as long as the learned form a special class which feeds on knowledge and lives the artificial life of the city, just so long will they be occupied only with the denial of fictions rather than their conversion into reality.

Criticism in philosophy is also a school, not a departure from it. Kantianism and neo-Kantianism are forms of scholasticism. The *Critique of Pure Reason* can be called science or philosophy only within the narrow limits of the artificial and un-unified experience of the study and laboratory. In the same way the *Critique of Practical Reason* can be called life only in the sense of life set within the narrow bounds of individual concerns, of division that is not regarded as a vice. It is a system of morality for the immature, according to which all crimes are simply pranks, which is just what the Russian people call them. The *Critique of Practical Reason* knows nothing of a united mankind; it gives no rules for the common action of the whole human race, just as the *Critique of Pure Reason* knows no experience other than that which is had *in some particular place, at some particular time, by some particular person*. It does not know the experience which is had *by all people everywhere and always*, as it will be when armed peoples (armies) convert their weapons into instruments for the regulation of atmospheric phenomena.

In the *Critique of Pure Reason* everything good, i.e., God, constitutes an ideal; in the *Critique of Practical Reason* it is an extra-worldly reality, while reality consists of: (a) the soulless world, an irrational and insentient power, for which "chaos" is a more appropriate term than "cosmos," while its study is more appropriately called "chaos-ography" than cosmology; and (b) the impotent soul, the study of which may be called psychology —in the sense of "psychocracy," but only a projective psychocracy, since apart from God and the world the soul is only the capability of feeling, knowing, and acting—it is a soul without any real power or will. Herein lies the separation of the soul from power and the world from reason and feeling; their unification can only be a project—something which is not to be found in Kant. If for idealists there is peace only beyond this world, while for materialists there is no peace either in this world or beyond it, for critical philosophy (Kant) peace exists only in our thought, and not in reality at all. When the illegitimacy of the separation of the intelligentsia from the common people is recognized, thought will become projective. Are we not justified in saying, therefore, that critical philosophy, like positivism, is a school, and that both positive and critical philosophy are forms of scholasticism belonging to the years of immaturity? . . .

The happiness in this life which Kant was able to give man was bought at a very great price: forget about the perfection which is unattainable (God is only the ideal) and your imperfection will not disturb you; don't think about death and you will not fall into the paralogism of thinking that immortality is real; be concerned only with the visible and don't think about the future: you cannot decide whether the world is finite or infinite, eternal or not eternal. This is Kant's position in the *Critique of Pure Reason.*

However, the whole negative doubt of the *Critique of Pure Reason* is based on the presumed inevitability of division among men and the impossibility of their unification in a common task. This presupposition is a prejudice completely unrecognized by Kant himself, one which the great philosopher evidently did not even suspect; and he did not suspect it precisely because he was a great philosopher and consequently was unable to set anything above thought. What Kant believed to be inaccessible to knowledge is the object of a task, but a task which is only within the reach of people taken together, in the combining of independent persons and not in their separateness and diversity. The *Critique of Practical Reason* is also based on the unconscious acknowledgment of the inevitability of division; the vice of division (not recognized as such, of course) is at the heart of Kant's ethical system. This philosopher belongs to the epoch of what has been called enlightened absolutism, and he has transferred the principles of this absolutism into the moral world; it is as if he was making God say: "Everything for people and nothing through people." The principle of division and inaction is asserted by Kant in all three of his critiques.[2] The philosophy of art, which he calls the critique of judgment, speaks not of how to create but only of how to judge objects of art and works of nature from the viewpoint of aesthetics. This is a philosophy for art critics and not for artists or poets, not even for artists taken separately, to say nothing of the time when they will be regarded as executors of a single work in contrast to the division and even hostility which exists among them now. In the critique of judgment, nature too is regarded not as the object of a task, of an action involving the transformation of blind force into a force governed by reason, but only as a subject of judgment and contemplation, and then only from the aesthetic rather than the moral viewpoint, in which it would appear as a destructive and death-dealing force.

14.

In limiting man to what is necessary, to existence itself, in reconciling itself with loss and death, positivism in all its forms

2. It would be truer to say that the principle of division and inaction is preached by Kant not just in three but in all four of his critiques, since religion too is confined as in a prison within the narrow limits of pure reason. Having condemned religion to prison for having wished to save the world from final destruction through a fulfillment of the duty of raising the dead, Kant then ordered that it be stripped of the weapons (science and art) with which it wished to attain its good end (eutelism), and these too were condemned to solitary confinement. Having committed this crime (unconsciously, of course), the philosopher-king was then certain that he had secured for mankind a quiet and untroubled end. But supramoralism is breaking down the prison walls and releasing the prisoners.

shows that it is very sympathetic to the artificial demands which do not secure our existence but simply stir up our desires. Thus in China the moral sense (love of children for their parents) manifests itself in the form of ceremony and games and is becoming more and more fictitious. Even the things brought for sacrifice are replaced by models or figures, while amusements and diversions are elevated to the level of a real and serious task, i.e., priority is in fact given to artificial requirements—while hypocritically the first place is given to the satisfaction of the moral sense. In Europe, on the contrary, things are frankly and openly valued above the dead—while hypocrisy appears in the claim that the living are valued above things. But if the struggle for existence, i.e., the struggle among people for the sake of things, is accepted as the condition of progress, then things as ends must be preferred to people as means. Each person will value others only as allies in the business of acquiring things.

Not only that, but in contrast to the popular view which sees things as animate, philosophy converts animate beings into things. "Each being can be apprehended by another only as matter, as a thing endowed with the power of movement. It can exist as spirit only for itself; only to itself can it appear as a spirit endowed with consciousness, sensation, and will." From which it follows that every being, having applied this critique to himself, can accept as highly probable the idea that he alone is a spirit and that all other beings are things. "About the existence of conscious states outside myself, in other beings, I can draw conclusions only by way of analogy; I perceive directly only the movements of other beings and not their inner state." The acceptance (by each person) of all other persons only as things and of oneself alone as a sentient and conscious being, i.e., the acceptance of the soul in oneself alone, the acceptance of oneself alone as a man, and the non-acceptance of all others similar to oneself as one's relatives, is the complete negation of morality, brotherhood, and fatherland-ness, that is, if philosophy has in general ever recognized a fatherland; really it recognizes no fathers and ignores the reality of a fatherland. The practical expression of such a theoretical philosophy will involve the real acceptance of a soul only in oneself and the real negation of souls in all others; i.e., an utter contempt for morality. But if men were completely sincere and other souls were not darkness, if it were possible to define infallibly the psychic state of others by their external movements, and, on the other hand, if we ourselves did not lead others astray by movements of our own which do not correspond to our psychic states, i.e., if it happened not only that other souls were not darkness to us but also that our own souls were not a deception for others, then it would be impossible to consider others as being unlike ourselves. It is just here that we have the application of psychology to life and the organization of society, if psychology is to have any application at all.

15.

Leaving both initiating [efficient] and final causes out of its purview, positivism believes it impossible to know the meaning and goals of life. The scholastic positivism of the learned class is a distortion of life; for positivists the raising of the dead is not only not possible, it is not even desirable. But by not desiring the restoration of their own life, do they not prove that their life is not worth restoring? For the progressivists, everything that exists is bad, while all that was and has passed away is even worse; and only for unreflective progressivists can that which does not yet exist appear to be good, since even the future is becoming the present and the past, i.e., bad. Thus it is clear that a true progressivist is inevitably a pessimist. "*Progress*," says one well-known professor,[3] "is the constant raising of the level of universal human development. In this sense we find the prototype of progress in individual psychic development, which is not only an objective fact of observation, but also a subjective fact of consciousness. In our inner experience development appears in the form of a consciousness of a constant increase of knowledge and clarification of thought, and these processes are perceived in the form of an improvement or elevation of our reflective nature. This fact of individual psychology

3. N. I. Kareyev.—TRANS.

is repeated in collective psychology when the members of a whole society recognize their own superiority over their fore-fathers in the same society." But society is made up of a younger and an older generation, of fathers and sons; and if by the term "a whole society" the author has in mind both the old and the young, if he has in mind people of all ages without any differentiation, in other words, if he assumes the equal mobility of all members of society (denying the process of aging and weakening), then a superiority will be acknowledged only over the dead, in which case the remembrance of the dead (history) will be necessary only in order to have someone to whom one can be superior.

So then a whole society (all the living, both young and old) can recognize its superiority only over the departed generations. But how can one fail to see the culpability of such a view, fail to notice the egoism of the present generation? The life of a society consists in the fact that what is old grows older and what is young grows up; in growing up and realizing its superiority over the dead, the younger generation cannot, according to the law of progress, fail to realize also its superiority over those who are growing old, who are dying. If the elder says to the younger: "It is for you to grow up and for me to decrease," this wish is a good one, fatherly love is speaking here. But if the younger says to the elder: "It is for me to grow up and for you to be laid in the tomb," this is progress, and it is not love speaking here but hatred, the hatred, of course, of prodigal sons.

In the absence of an inner unification and an outer common task for the whole human race, progress is a natural phenomenon. Until there is full unity in the common task of transforming death-dealing forces into life-giving ones, man will be subjected to blind natural force, on a level with cattle and all other beasts, on a level with soulless matter.

Progress originates in the doctrine of redemption, but by way of a complete distortion of this doctrine. Prior to its ultimate distortion by Protestantism, redemption referred primarily to the dead, while progress is self-exaltation, the exaltation of oneself, that same sin which was punished by the confusion of tongues.

We have come close to this in our own time, when people are rejecting everything that is common and each person lives exclusively for himself, and this to such an extent that people cease even to understand one another. Progress consists in the sense of superiority, first, of a whole generation (the living) over their forefathers (the dead), and second, of the younger over the older generation, in which case this superiority—a matter of pride for the younger generation—will consist in the increase of knowledge, in the improvement and elevation of the thinking being. Even the development of moral convictions will be an occasion for the younger generation's self-exaltation over the older. "He (each member of the younger generation) feels his exaltation (his superiority over the older) when he is enriched with new knowledge, when he evolves a new idea, when he evaluates his environment from a new viewpoint, when in the collision of duty with habit and emotion victory is on the side of duty." [4]

But this is only the subjective, inner side of the sense of intellectual superiority over the forefathers; the professor is silent about the external side of this sense, about how this sense is expressed as an objective, observable fact for the forefathers who have not yet died. And yet the arrogant way that sons and daughters deal with their parents is sufficiently well known and has even found expression in the work of the author of *Fathers and Sons*, although this is not a very vivid representation of the situation.

It is impossible not to notice that if, in Western Europe, France and Germany are now the younger generation, nowhere has the antagonism of the younger against the older reached such an extreme as it has with us; hence for us it is easier than for others truly to evaluate the doctrine of progress. . . . Biologically, progress consists in the swallowing up of the old by the new, in the displacing of the fathers by the sons. Sociologically, progress is expressed in the attainment of the fullest measure of freedom accessible to man, not in the greatest

4. This quotation is from Kareyev; the parenthetical remarks are Fyodorov's.—TRANS.

participation of each person in the common filial task, since society as non-brotherhood requires a limitation of the freedom of each individual. Thus the demand of sociology will be a demand for the greatest freedom and the least unity and communion, i.e., sociology is the science not of association but of dissociation or enslavement [*razobshcheniye ili poraboshcheniye*], if society is allowed to swallow up the individual. As the science of dissociation for some people and the science of enslavement for others, sociology sins against both indivisibility and unconfusability [*nesliyannost*], against the Triune God.

. . . Although stagnation is death and regression is no paradise, progress is. a real hell, and the truly divine, truly human task is to save the victims of progress, to take them out of hell. As the negation of fatherland and brotherhood, progress is utter moral degeneration, the actual negation of morality. . . .

Thus progress consists in the sons' sense of superiority over their fathers, and in the sense of superiority of the living over the dead—a view which excludes the necessity and thus also the possibility of the unification of the living (sons) for the raising to life of the dead (fathers). However, the real superiority of the sons would be expressed in the task of raising the fathers to life, if indeed this could be called "superiority," while their self-exaltation over their forefathers is only an imaginary superiority. . . .

Progress transforms fathers and forefathers into accused prisoners, and gives judgment and dominion over them into the hands of their sons and descendants. Historians are judges over the dead, that is, over those who have already suffered the supreme punishment, the death penalty. The sons are also judges over those who have not yet died.

Of course, the learned are able to say that in former times the aged were killed while now they are only despised; isn't it progress to replace physical murder by spiritual murder?! The progress of progress itself, one might say! But in the future still greater improvements are to be expected of progress, i.e., contempt will gradually be decreased. And yet it is obvious that contempt can be eliminated only with the elimination of progress itself. Even with its improvement, that is, by its elimination, progress can only lead to a negative result, to the elimination of contempt, and not to love and respect for one's forefathers, not to feelings which elevate the descendants themselves. Can progress give meaning to life, to say nothing of purpose? For only that in which the highest degree of love and respect can be expressed gives both meaning and purpose to life.

Progress is the direct opposite of the raising of the dead. Progress consists in the critical attitude of the younger generation toward the older, in the condemnation of fathers by their sons, and in action which accords with such condemnation. "The goal of progress is the developed and ever-developing individual, or the fullest measure of freedom attainable by man." In other words, the goal of progress, as we have said, is not community but disunity, so that the lowest level of brotherhood is also the expression of the highest progress. Thus in condemning the human race to eternal division and non-brotherhood, the learned professor also signs a death warrant for the learned as a class, not, however, as a commission or task force for the investigation of the causes of nature's dis-relatedness with man, leading to the removal of these causes, to the controlling of nature's forces. As long as knowledge is regarded as an end in itself and the learned see themselves as the best and highest class, just so long will the question of dis-relatedness and of the restoration of relatedness fail to be set forth in all its force and meaning.

The specialization of the learned has its temporary significance; the conversion of the commission of the learned into a class is the same abuse which we see in the conversion of a dictatorship into a tyranny. The acceptance of knowledge as an end in itself, the replacement of work by *Weltanschauung*— "ideolatry" or the cult of ideas—is the legitimation of this abuse. Religion, in the Platonic sense of the raising of the dead without man's participation in this task, is the sanction of this abuse. . . . The learned professor ascribes the greatest significance to knowledge as an end in itself, to pure knowledge as a spiritual interest, and he even regards its inapplicability as a merit: "Man shall not live by bread alone," he (Kareyev) says, completely ignoring the all-embracing question of life and death, the question of the material conditions on which man's existence depends.[5] . . .

The raising of the dead is not progress, but it requires a real improvement, a true perfection. Nor is there any need for that which is self-generating or which proceeds out of itself, either in the reason or the will (if we avoid confusing the latter with appetite). The raising of the dead is the replacement of the lust to engender by conscious re-creation. Any other kind of progress is artificial, arbitrary, contrived—neither natural nor inevitable. When it is equated with development or evolution,

5. But there can be no knowledge without application; if knowledge has no application to work then it manifests itself in self-exaltation. Drawing conclusions from all that has been written about the philosophy of history, Kareyev thinks he finds a point on which all, or nearly all, philosophers are agreed. On the strength of this agreement he is now creating a new science under the not entirely new name of "Historiosophy." This science, which might more accurately be called "Historiosophistry," is in fact completely opposed to history, which has as its goal the unification of the living (sons) for the raising to life of the dead (fathers). The point on which the philosophers are supposed to be agreed is "progress," which in Kareyev's opinion is the very thing which gives meaning to history. Progress (forward movement, improvement) apparently has significance not only for future generations, but also for those that are past—"for all people in general, wherever they may be, whenever they may have lived," says our historiosophist. From history, as it is given to us in experience, he draws conclusions—by way of historiosophistry—not only about social progress but also about psychic progress in inter-personal relations, although psychology and sociology remain sciences sharply set apart one from the other. (But if the soul were to be improved there would be love, and society would be a brotherhood of sons, i.e., the full expression of love; and psychology and sociology would then be transformed into psychocracy.) For Kareyev, progress is the supreme criterion for judging history—the philosophy of history is, after all, judgment—and it is in progress that the significance of history is to be found. But if we take the raising of the dead as the criterion, then we shall see that insofar as it involves redemption it excludes judgment above all things. If it is adopted as a criterion, the raising of the dead need not be disputed, it can afford not to refute the assertion that the happiness of later generations is founded on the unhappiness of those who have gone before. But the raising of the dead cannot be limited to a negative good; it not only negates the unhappiness of preceding generations, it also demands their happiness.

progress is clearly a concept borrowed from blind nature and applied to human life. But if we accept the forward movement from worse to better as progress, if we accept the idea that the verbal animal is better and higher than the non-verbal, can we then take the latter as the model for the former, can we conceive of blind unconscious force as a model for that which has feeling and consciousness? As a transition from worse to better, progress of course requires that the inadequacies of blind nature be corrected by that nature which is conscious of them, i.e., by the combined power of the human race. It requires

---

Historiosophy is not historical wisdom, not a philosophy which teaches people what they must do together. If historical wisdom is unable to see a general plan in history, this is not for the same reason that historiosophistry fails to see such a plan. To see a plan means to ascribe a planned-ness to our actions, means not to admit the division in which we are living, not to admit our egoism, and at the same time it means to refuse to unite for the common task. Historiosophistry destroys the wheat with the tares, since it does not acknowledge or at any rate does not think about unity. The central thing in the philosophy of history is not unification, not the unity of persons, but their division, for, after all, the conceptual abstraction from all particular societies does not eliminate division. Only the raising of the dead can be a transition to a common, yet specific task. A subjective sympathy is powerless against reality and, most important, it is useless—unless it becomes a task. If it does become a task then the subjective is at once transformed into the projective. In acknowledging individuality as the central object of the philosophy of history, historiosophistry leaves unification to the operation of blind force. But history as wisdom, as a moral undertaking, is the unification in the common task of raising the dead. For the learned, history is the restoration of the past; for the people, it is *the raising of the dead*, although this is still only in the phase of mythical art, since the people still do not possess knowledge, since even today knowledge is separated from action. "History is made up of the actions of individuals (solitary individuals) and this must be the basic principle of historiosophy." However, the activity of individuals does not create history, but rather the comedy of world history. That history which is created, according to the principle of historiosophistry, by solitary individuals, is really the struggle of these individuals for the right to lead the crowd toward a goal or ideal which serves only as a decoy for ensnaring the people. The true wisdom of history consists not in being separated, or being freed from traditions, in replacing them by personal caprice, but in understanding them, with a view to remaining in harmony with the masses; it involves turning the mythical task into one that is actual and common to all.

that improvement through conflict and destruction be replaced
by a restoration of the victims of this conflict. In this way
progress will not be the improvement of goals only, but also of
means. Such improvement would be not just an improvement or
correction, but the eradication of evil and the planting of good
in its place.

Progress itself requires the raising of the dead, but such a
requirement consists of progress not in knowledge only, but
also in action, a progress in knowledge not just of *what is* but
also of *what ought to be*. Only with the passage of the learned
class out of knowledge into work will progress pass from knowledge of *what is* to knowledge of *what ought to be*.

Nothing so clearly demonstrates the true nature of progress,
of this hurried movement toward novelty and hasty negation of
antiquity, of this unthinking replacement of the old by the new,
than paleography, the science of ancient and modern forms of
writing which bear the imprint of the transition from the old
cult of the fathers to the new cult of the wives. The displacement of the former for the sake of the latter is reflected in
these forms, for literature is simply the graphic representation
of the progress of that being which has been endowed with
speech. Although it is a humble science, paleography can therefore be the accuser of proud progress. As it studies the forms
of letters, or literally, as it pursues its pedantry [*bukvoyedstvo* =
"letter-eating"], this science is much despised by certain progressivists, and yet the forms of letters say much more than
the words, and they speak more sincerely. The forms of letters
cannot be corrupted as words can. The words of written script,
for example, speak of progress, but the forms of the letters, as
we shall see, show a regression. Pedantry actually gives paleography the opportunity to define the character of epochs, turning it into an art or skill which by tracing the changes in
handwriting reveals the variations of mood which have occurred
in the spirit of different generations, including variations in
essential characteristics, such as shifts from faith and piety to
doubt, unbelief, and secularness. Faith or piety is expressed in a
reverence based on the awareness of one's imperfection, one's
mortality, while doubt or unbelief is expressed in the feeling of

contempt which begins with contempt toward past generations (toward the dead) and the forgetting of one's own mortality, and ends with the complete dis-valuing of life, i.e., pessimism, Buddhism. The goal of paleography is to define not the character of persons, but the character of societies, the level of their elevation or decline.

The name of the handwriting which prevailed in the Middle Ages is Gothic, the same name used for the architecture of those churches which united all the arts, and which were built up over many centuries, so that only the descendants of those who began the construction of these churches ever saw their completion. This name, as applied to all aspects of life, shows what a close connection there is between the forms of letters and the whole life of this period. Thus too in the case of ancient Russia, Byzantine Russia; the names used for the handwriting of that period [*Ustavny* or *Poluustavny*] use the same term which describes the established order [*ustav*] to which the whole life of the time, both religious and secular, was subjected. Gothic and "Ustavny" letters, traced out with deep reverence, with love, even with delight, and executed like works of art, like prayers (of course not like present-day prayer, concerned as it is with petitioning for a thousand and one benefits), and produced with the same feelings with which churches were built and ikons were painted in this epoch—these letters were something magnificent, like the Gothic cathedrals, and did not, of course, have that womanish beauty which prevails now in the epoch of the cult of woman. Sharply distinguished from one another, since they were produced neither hurriedly nor impatiently, they were produced as a labor which was viewed as a blessing, not a curse . . . to say nothing of a heavenly reward. Hoping for blessedness in the future, these copyists had a foretaste of it in the present in the delight they found in the labor itself. But now progressivists see in Gothic letters only the backwardness of a time when people traveled by ox-cart, or an immovability, so despised by progress, since progress is itself a change [*izmeneniye*], a movement, and in the moral sense a betrayal [*izmena*]. While in Ustavny letters they see not only what is hostile to progress (to what is moved by constant dissatisfaction and unrest), not only a hated backwardness, stagnation, unchangeability, but also slavery, the absence of freedom, i.e., the restraint of personal inclinations, the restraint of movement and action. . . .

In calling the letters of modern times "rapid," [6] by suggesting a property which belongs also to rapid-fire weapons, automatic printing presses, and can be applied to means of rapid transportation, this term catches the most essential feature or property of modern times. The concept of progress includes not simply the concept of change and movement but also that of constantly accelerating motion. "Rapid" can be applied to everything that exists in modern times. This definition may be applied even to literature, which is a speed-writing [*skoropisaniye* = "shorthand"], and thanks to speed [*skorost*] is also becoming a multiple-writing [*mnogopisaniye*], i.e., quantitatively but not qualitatively abundant. Present-day industry too may be called "rapid-making," but the rapidity in this case is leading to overproduction on the one hand, and to the impermanence of products on the other. This rapidity deprives all work, not only mechanical but also intellectual work, of artistic attractiveness, turning it into a means of profit without any goal whatever, unless sense pleasure is to be considered a goal. If Gothic and Ustavny lettering furnish pleasure, then cursive writing [*skoropis*], and everything to which the word "rapid" has been prefixed, can scarcely be taken as objects of pleasure. Thus the present generation is not only deprived of felicity in the present but also expects none in the future.

Moved by dissatisfaction, which is the enemy of immovability and unchangeability and therefore also of faith and dogmatism, progress can be nothing but criticism in thought and reform or revolution in life—that is, if it is not simply evolution.

In very recent times even cursive writing has seemed too slow, and shorthand has been created for the copying out of everything written in longhand. Cursive writing, in spite of its rapidity, still leaves a certain freedom to the copyist; now the

6. The Russian word here is *skory*, which in this context would normally be translated "cursive," except that this would destroy the sense of Fyodorov's play on words in the whole passage that follows.—TRANS.

stenographer, who is in complete dependence on the one who is speaking, is transformed into a machine or phonograph. To understand the essence of progress you have to see the whole path from painting [*zhivopis*] as the first form of writing, requiring artistic abilities and fullness of soul in the writer (as in hieroglyphics, a form of live writing [*zhivoye pismo*] which spoke primarily of the dead and as it were animated them) down to shorthand writing, in which there is no painting at all. Shorthand is "dead writing" [*mertvopis*] that speaks of the trifles of the living and is carried out by a man who has been turned into an automatic writing-machine.

Let us assume that speed is necessary because life is short, and the age of cursive writing or shorthand knows no other life, or acknowledges such a life less and less and denies it more and more. And yet speed does not fill the soul; instead, it empties it, since progress sacrifices the soul for the sake of increasing the size and number of objects of sense pleasure, for the sake of multiplying not the objects of necessity but the objects of luxury. The ideal of progress (according to the concept of the learned) is that all might share in both the production and use of objects of sense pleasure, while the goal of true progress can and must be only the sharing of all in the task or work of coming to know the blind force which brings famine, plague, and death, in order to convert it into a force which brings life. Instead of this, instead of transforming the blind force of nature into a force governed by reason, progress turns the soul itself into a blind force.

16.

The doctrine of raising the dead can perhaps be called positivism, but it is completely opposed to progress as the displacing of the older generation by the younger, as the exaltation of the sons over the fathers, and it is also opposed to positivism understood as knowledge only, as a school, as a form of scholasticism. The doctrine of raising the dead may be called positivism, but it is a positivism of action, since according to this doctrine mythical knowledge is not replaced by positive knowledge, but mythical, fictitious action is replaced by positive and real action.

At the same time, the doctrine of the raising of the dead does not set arbitrary limits to action and has in view a common action and not the action of separate individuals. The raising of the dead, as an action, is a positivism in the sphere of final causes; while positivism in the usual sense, i.e., positivism of knowledge, refers to the realm of initiating or efficient causes. However, the positivism of final causes does not exclude the positivism of efficient causes. . . . Positivism of action (the doctrine of the raising of the dead) has as its forerunner not mythology but mythical art, since mythology is the product of a special class of sacrificial priests, while the common people have their cult, their sacrifices, their mythical art, and the raising of the dead is the conversion of this into art that is actual.

Positivism of action is not something belonging to a class, but something belonging to all the people. Science will be its instrument. On the other hand, positivism of knowledge is nothing more than the philosophy of the learned as a special class or hierarchy. A positivism which does not set arbitrary limits to action, but which recognizes what were initiating or efficient causes in the final causes or results of action, has a different origin than the positivism which limits both knowledge and action. It does not stem from the loss of hope, nor from the desire to be reconciled with evil for the sake of enjoying the present, nor from the desire for repose in old age; or if it stems from a loss, it is the loss of superstition. The learned positivism, however, while it limits the task of the human race, does not consider it necessary to indicate the reasons for such a limitation. In this connection it is not only uncritical, it is positively superstitious. Positivism in theory has its foundation in the so-called positivity of life, and consists in the renunciation of the struggle against the fundamental evil which comes as a result of fatigue or feebleness, or as the result of the wish to surrender to pleasure instead of work. This is not humility before the Divine will (which they do not accept, or rather do not wish to know, and which in any case cannot be represented as making such an evil command), but simply a debased worship of blind force.

Since it is the opposite of progress considered as the sense of superiority of the young over the old and as the displacing of the older by the younger, the raising of the dead requires an education which does not arm the sons against the fathers, but rather establishes the raising to life of the fathers as the main task of the sons. It requires an education which would be the fulfillment of the prophecy of Malachi, the last Old Testament prophet, an education which would be a mutual turning of the hearts of the fathers to the sons and of the sons to the fathers. True education consists not in the sense of superiority over the fathers, but in the consciousness of the fathers in oneself, and of oneself in them. The raising of the dead is the full expression of maturity, it is the departure from school, and it requires a society of independent persons, of sons, who are participating in the common task of raising the forefathers from the dead. The task of the fathers or parents ends with the end of upbringing, and then begins the task of the sons, of those who restore life. In giving birth to their children and in raising them, the parents give up their whole life to them, while the restoration of life to the fathers (which is also the expression of maturity) begins with the task of raising the dead.

17.

Positivism was right in regarding knowledge critically and saying that it is incapable of resolving fundamental questions; but the knowledge it was criticizing was only a class knowledge, it was only knowledge and not action, which ought not to be and in fact cannot be separated from knowledge. Aristotle can be considered as the father of the learned class, and yet we ascribe to this philosopher such a saying as: "We know only what we ourselves do," a statement which clearly does not permit a separation of knowledge from action, i.e., the isolation of the learned as a special class. And yet, even though more than two thousand years have passed since Aristotle's time, there has not been one thinker who has placed this principle, this criterion, this testing of knowledge by action, at the heart of his doctrine. What then would one's own knowledge of the external world (nature—both past and present) signify, if not a project for the transformation of what is born or given in life into that which is earned by labor, together with the restoration of power and life to those who gave birth? This would be a project for the transformation of blind force into rational force, and the actualization of this project would demonstrate that life is not an accidental or useless gift.

Equally justified was the criticism of personal, individual reason, the reason of people taken in isolation. This criticism would have been completely justified if only it had involved the demand for a transition out of class knowledge (consisting in the clash of opinions out of which truth is supposed to proceed) into all-embracing knowledge, to the unification of the individual powers of all people in one common task. But instead of that the learned positivism, by denying the necessity of universal unification, has only led to a schism within the learned class itself, has led to its division into positivists and metaphysicians.

The learned are right in saying that the world is an idea or representation, since as learned people they have an exclusively cognitive relation with the world. But such a concept of the world belongs to one class only, and by no means to the whole human race, and so the learned are not right when by speaking this way they reject action, replacing it by knowledge, and even reject the possibility of acting. The learned are not right when they do not admit the projective within the subjective.

When contemporary monism says that it "reconciles spirit and matter in a higher unity, as two manifestations of one and the same hidden essence, apprehended subjectively (in inner experience) as spirit and objectively (in external experience) as matter," it is evident that such a reconciliation or unity is completely imaginary and has no real significance. "The anthropopathic monism of primitive man, and the mechanistic monism of modern science—here we see the point of departure and the last word in the history of man's view of the world." But a mechanistic world view can be a last word only for soulless people, for the learned, for positivists, since the notion of the world as a soulless mechanism inevitably invites attempts to make the mechanism the instrument of will, reason, and feeling. If primitive mankind stubbornly spiritualized matter and materialized spirit, the new man will strive no less stubbornly toward the real control of blind force. Here we have the true conversion of the mythical into the positive.

If positivism, like knowledge in general, is still spoken of as an activity, this is not because progress in language lags behind progress in thought (can inactivity be perfection?!!), but because man is by nature a doer. The savage expresses himself and the world precisely as they ought to be—i.e., himself as active and the world as living. The mistake of the positivists consists in the fact that they consider themselves above the savage in every respect, and that they apprehend the world and themselves as they ought not to be, and thus are unable to eliminate the contradiction between language and thought. (When a learned person of this or that school speaks of his operations of thought or knowledge as actions, or of the restoration of the past in the realm of thought as the raising of the dead, he is speaking metaphorically.) . . .

18.

As long as the learned or the philosophers remain a class the question of morality or of a task will be for them a question of knowledge only and not of action, will be a subject of study only and not an application of knowledge to life, and the task will be something that happens of its own accord instead of something that *ought* to be done, and done not in isolation but by all together. If the learned are not yet able to transform themselves from a class into a commission or task force for the development of a general plan of action (and without this the human race cannot act as one man according to a general plan, i.e., will not attain its maturity), the contradiction between the reflective and the instinctive cannot be resolved. Not having accepted work as its own task, the learned class remains reflective, while the human race—not yet united for common action—remains the instrument of blind force, acting instinctively. Reflection can only have a destructive effect on the human race, and it replaces what is destroyed with nothing. "To be the conscious agent of the evolution of the universe" means to become a conscious instrument for mutual crowding (conflict) and displacing (death); it means to subordinate the moral to the physical. And yet man, even in the midst of his present division and ineffective knowledge, in some way expresses moral demands as he yields to necessity out of physical weakness.

As long as division and inaction are not accepted as being

temporary, we are in no position even to imagine the scope and significance of the highest good. That state which Spencer and in particular his followers are promising mankind in the future cannot be accepted as the highest, or even as the very lowest, good. On the contrary, such a state, as the conversion of conscious activity into instinctive, automatic activity, as the conversion of man into a machine (which is in fact the ideal of blind fatalistic progress), is to be viewed as the very greatest evil. "The day is coming," says Spencer, "when the altruistic inclination will be so well implanted in our organism that people will vie with each other for opportunities of sacrifice and death." But if such an altruistic inclination is implanted in everyone, how will there be an occasion for its application? Such a condition presupposes the existence of oppressors, torturers, tyrants; either that or the common need to sacrifice oneself must produce benefactors who will become torturers and oppressors simply to satisfy the terrible need of others to become martyrs. Or else, finally, nature itself will remain a blind force in order to fulfill the role of executioner. If life is a good, then its sacrifice will be the loss of a good for those who have given up their lives for others; but then will life be good for those who have accepted the sacrifice and preserved their life at the expense of another's death? How is altruism possible without egoism? Those who sacrifice their lives are altruists; but those who accept the sacrifice . . . what are they? And if life is not a good, then, from the viewpoint of the one giving his life, there is no sacrifice or good work involved in giving it up.

If knowledge is separated from action, as is the case in the science and scholarship of the learned class, then what is done instinctively, in becoming conscious, destroys itself: "if morality is the instinct which moves an individual to sacrifice himself for the sake of the species, then morality is the love of those who have been born for those who gave birth to them, then the consciousness of one's origin, connected as it is with the death of one's parents, will not stop at knowledge but will also pass on to the task of raising the dead."

19.

The question of non-brotherhood, of dis-unity, and of the means of restoring relatedness in all its fullness and power (to the point of visibleness, obviousness) and the question of the unification of sons (brotherhood) for the raising to life of the fathers (full and complete relatedness) are of course identical, and are both opposed to progress or eternal immaturity, i.e., to the inability to restore life to the fathers, the incapacity for attaining moral and not just physical maturity, the latter not really being maturity at all. The second formulation of this question, however, i.e., the question of unification for the raising of the dead, is the more definite of the two. To outline this question even more clearly it is necessary to add that this unification of sons for the raising to life of the fathers is the fulfillment not simply of our own will but also the will of the God of our fathers, who is also not alien to us. This gives a true goal and meaning to life; in it there is expressed precisely the duty of the sons of man; and it is the result of "knowledge of all things by all men" and not a class knowledge. In it—in re-creation, in the replacement of birth-giving by the raising of the dead, of upbringing by creativity—we are looking for the purest (immortal) felicity, and not for mere comfort. In this form the question of dis-relatedness is opposed also to socialism, which misuses the word "brotherhood" and openly rejects the concept of fatherland.

At the present time socialism has no opponents; religions, with their transcendence, their "not of this world," and their "the Kingdom of God is within you," are unable to withstand it. Socialism can even appear to be an actualization of Christian morality. It is precisely the question of the unification of sons in the name of the fathers which is needed to expose the complete immorality of unity in the name of progress and comfort, a unity which displaces the fathers. Unification in the name of comfort and for the sake of one's own pleasure is the worst abuse of life, intellectually, aesthetically, and especially morally. When fathers are forgotten by their own sons, art is transformed from the purest felicity experienced in the restoring of life to the fathers into a pornocratic delight, while science is transformed from knowledge by all the living of everything nonliving (for the restoration of life to the dead) into the invention of pleasures or fruitless speculation. Socialism is triumphing over the state, over religion, and over science. The appearance of state socialism, of Catholic, Protestant, and "academic" socialism, bears witness to this triumph. It not only has no opponents, but also does not even admit their possibility. Socialism is a lie; it gives the name of relatedness, brotherhood, to the "comradely" association of people who are strangers to one another and are connected only by the external ties of utility, while real blood relatedness connects people by an inner feeling. The feeling of relatedness cannot be limited to representation of persons [*litse-predstavleniye*], it requires insight into persons [*litsezreniye*]. Death converts insight into persons into representation of persons, and so the sense of relatedness requires the restoration of the dead person. As far as it is concerned, the dead person is irreplaceable, while as far as "comrades" are concerned, death is a loss which can be made entirely good.

Unification, not for the achievement of comfort and material satisfaction for all the living, but for the raising to life of the dead, requires universal (compulsory) education which will reveal the character and ability of each person and will show each person *what* he must do and *with whom*—beginning with marriage. He must bear his burden in the task of transforming the blind force of nature into one controlled by reason, in the work of converting it from a death-dealing into a life-giving force. Is it possible, is it even natural to limit the "human task" to the mere maintaining of the proper distribution of the products of industry, forcing each person to take care, unfeelingly and dispassionately, that no one appropriate more than others or that no one sacrifice anything to others? Although socialism has been called into being artificially, socialists are careful to take advantage of the natural weaknesses of man. Thus in Germany they reproached the German workers for the limitedness of their demands, pointing to the English workers who were much more capricious; they also reproached them for their excessive love of work, inciting them to demand a reduction of working hours and days. Socialists, who think only about their own dvancement and not about the welfare of the people, pay no ttention to the fact that a cooperative state must have not the ices which they are promoting but the virtues, the fulfillment f duty, even self-sacrifice. In modern industrial states the work n industry may be light for the most part, but the existence of actories is maintained by the forced labor of miners who dig oal and iron; they are the necessary condition for the existence f industry. Under such conditions it is not an economic reform hat is needed, but a radical technological reform, or rather not ust a reform, but a universal transformation involving a trans- ormation of morality as well. The need for forced labor for he sake of universal comfort is an anomaly—even if this labor e equally distributed. Such a need may be thinkable for the ake of attaining brotherhood and fatherlandness, but only as a emporary measure.

With regulation of the meteorological process energy will be drawn from the atmosphere, coal will be replaced by that same nergy out of which the supply of energy was derived in the orm of coal, and to which it will in any case have to return, ince the supply of coal is being steadily exhausted. The same nergy that is taken out of the atmospheric currents will cer- ainly produce a transformation in the process of obtaining iron n metallic form. Regulation is also necessary for the uniting of manufacturing and agriculture, since the excess of solar heat cting destructively in the air currents in gales and hurricanes an be utilized in the handcraft industry and will give an oppor- unity to spread this industry over the whole earth instead of concentrating it at certain points as it is today. The regulator lso transforms agriculture from an individual into a collective vork. In this way the regulator will mean not only (1) the end of var, but also (2) the replacing of the harsh forced labor of niners, (3) the unification of small handcraft industry with griculture, (4) the transformation of agriculture from individ- al into collective production, and in addition it will be a general nstrument for agriculture, and (5) it will be the transformation f agriculture from a means of obtaining a "maximum" income, omething which leads to crises and overproduction, into the hance of obtaining a "true" income. The call for regulation is eing raised therefore on all sides.

The nineteenth century is approaching its mournful and gloomy end; it moves neither toward light nor toward joy. It is already possible to give it a name. In contrast to the so-called age of enlightenment and philanthropy (the eighteenth century), in contrast also to the preceding centuries, beginning with the epoch of the Renaissance, it can be called the age of the revival of prejudices and superstitions, and of the denial of philanthropy and humanism. But it is not reviving those superstitions which in the Middle Ages alleviated life and aroused hope. Instead, it is reviving the superstitions which in those ages made life unbearable. The nineteenth century has revived faith in evil and renounced faith in goodness. It has renounced the Kingdom of Heaven and abandoned faith in earthly happiness or the Kingdom on Earth, which was an article of faith in the age of the Renaissance and in the eighteenth century. The nineteenth century is not only a century of revival of superstitions, but also, as we have said above, of the denial of philanthropy and humanism, something that is especially evident in the doctrines of contemporary criminologists. Having denied philanthropy and adopted Darwinism, the present century has accepted conflict as a legitimate task and instead of being simply a blind instrument of nature it has become its conscious instrument or organ. The armaments of the present day are completely in accord with the beliefs of the century, and only backward people who would like to appear advanced are—despite their Darwinism—denouncing war.

At the same time the nineteenth century is a direct descendant a true son of the preceding centuries, the direct consequence of the dividing of what is heavenly from what is earthly, of the complete distortion of Christianity, whose Covenant involves precisely the uniting of the heavenly and the earthly, the divine and the human. The universal immanent raising of the dead, a task pursued with all one's heart, with all one's mind, with all one's actions—a raising of the dead accomplished by means of all the powers and capabilities of all the sons of man such is the fulfillment of this Covenant of Christ, the Son of God and the Son of Man.

THE ESCHATOLOGICAL
AND PROPHETIC CHARACTER
OF RUSSIAN THOUGHT

Nicholas Berdyaev

The eschatological and prophetic character of Russian thought. The Russian people are a people of the End. Apocalypsis among the masses and in the cultured class. The Reality of Russian Messianism, its distortion by imperialism. The rejection of the bourgeois virtues among the Russian people. The people's searchers after the Kingdom of God. Distorted eschatology among the revolutionary Intelligentsia. Russian expectation of the revelation of the Holy Spirit. Eschatology and Messianism in Dostoyevsky. Outbursts in V. Solovëv and K. Leontyev. The genius of Fedorov's idea about the conditionality of eschatological prophecy. The problem of birth and death in Solovëv, Rozanov and Fedorov. Three currents in Orthodoxy

I

I wrote in my book on Dostoyevsky that the Russians are apocalyptics or nihilists. The Russian is an apocalyptic revolt against antiquity (Spengler). This means that the Russian people, in accordance with their metaphysical nature and vocation in the world are a people of the End. Apocalypse has always played a great part both among the masses of our people and at the highest cultural level, among Russian writers and thinkers. In our thought the eschatological problem takes an immeasurably greater place than in the thinking of the West and this is connected with the very structure of Russian consciousness which is but little adapted and little inclined to cling to finished forms of the intervening culture. Positivist historians may point out that in order to sketch the character of the Russian people I make a selection. I select the few, the exceptional, whereas the many, the usual have been different. But an intellectually attainable picture of a people can only be sketched by way of selection, which intuitively penetrates into what is most expressive and significant. I have laid stress all the while upon the prophetic element in Russian literature and thought of the nine-

teenth century. I have spoken also 'of the part which the eschatological mentality has played in the Russian schism and sectarian life.
The academic and administrative element has either been very weak
among us, almost absent, or it has been horrible and abominable as
in the 'Domostroi'. The books on ethical teaching by Bishop
Theophan Zatvornik have also a rather degrading character, but this
is connected with the rooted Russian dualism, with the evil powers
which organize the earth and earthly life, powers which have
abandoned the truth of Christ. The forces of good seek for the city
which is to come, the Kingdom of God. The Russian people have
many gifts, but the gift of form is comparatively weak among them.
A strong elemental force overthrows every kind of form, and it is
this which to Western people, and especially to the French, among
whom primitive elementalism has almost disappeared, appears to be
barbarous. In Western Europe civilization which has attained great
heights, more and more excludes eschatological thought. Roman
Catholic thought fears the eschatological interpretation of Christianity since it opens up the possibility of dangerous innovations. The
spirit which strives towards the world which is to come, the messianic expectation, is incompatible with the academic socially-
organized character of Roman Catholicism; it evokes fears that the
possibility of the direction of souls might be weakened. In the same
way bourgeois society, believing in nothing whatever, fears that
eschatological thought might loosen the foundations of that bourgeois society. Léon Bloy, that rarity in France, a writer of the apocalyptic spirit, was hostile to bourgeois society and bourgeois civilization; they had no liking for him and set little value upon him.[1] In
years of catastrophe the apocalyptic mentality has made its appearance in European society. Such was the case after the French Revolution and the Napoleonic wars.[2] At that time Jung-Stilling prophesied
the near appearance of antichrist. In the most distant past, in the
ninth century in the West there was the expectation of antichrist.
Nearer to the Russians were the prophecies of Joachim of Floris

[1] See L. Bloy's amazing book, *Exégèse des lieux communs*. It is a terrible exposure
of the bourgeois spirit and of bourgeois wisdom.
[2] Much interesting material is to be found in A. Wiatte, *Les sources occultes du
romantisme*, 2 volumes.

about a new era of the Holy Spirit, an era of love, friendship and freedom, although all this was too much associated with monachism. The figure of Saint·Francis of Assisi has close affinities with the Russians, Saint Francis who redeemed many of the sins of historical Christianity. But the Christian civilization of the West was organized outside the sphere of eschatological expectation. I must explain what I understand by eschatology. I have in mind not the eschatological section of theological Christianity which one can find in every course on theology, whether Catholic or Protestant; I have in mind the eschatological interpretation of Christianity as a whole, which must be opposed to the historical interpretation of Christianity. The Christian revelation is an eschatological revelation, a revelation of the end of this world, a revelation of the Kingdom of God. The whole of primitive Christianity was eschatological. It expected the second Advent of Christ and the coming of the Kingdom of God.[1] Historical Christianity and the Church of history indicate failure in the sense that the Kingdom of God has not come; they indicate failure, owing to the accommodation of Christian revelation to the kingdom of this world. There remains, therefore, in Christianity the messianic hope, the eschatological expectation, and it is stronger in Russian Christianity than in the Christianity of the West. The Church is not the Kingdom of God; the Church has appeared in history and it has acted in history; it does not mean the transfiguration of the world, the appearance of a new heaven and a new earth. The Kingdom of God is the transfiguration of the world, not only the transfiguration of the individual man, but also the transfiguration of the social and the cosmic; and that is the end of this world, of the world of wrong and ugliness, and it is the principle of a new world, a world of right and beauty. When Dostoyevsky said that beauty would save the world he had in mind the transfiguration of the world and the coming of the Kingdom of God, and this is the eschatological hope; it existed in the greater number of representatives of Russian religious thought. But Russian messianic consciousness like Russian eschatology was two-fold.

In Russian messianism, which was so characteristic of the Russian

[1] The eschatological interpretation of Christianity is to be found in Weiss and Loisy.

people, the pure messianic idea of the Kingdom of God, the kingdom of right, was clouded by the imperialistic idea, by the will to power. We have seen this already in relation to the notion of Moscow as the Third Rome. And in Russian communism in which the Russian messianic idea has passed into a non-religious and antireligious form, there has taken place the same distortion by the will to power, of the Russian quest for the kingdom of right. But the repudiation of the majesty and the glory of this world is very characteristic of the Russians in spite of all the seductive temptations to which they have been exposed; such at least they are in their finest moments. The majesty and glory of the world remain to them a seduction and a sin, and not as among Western peoples, the highest value. It is a characteristic fact that rhetoric is not natural to the Russians; there was absolutely none of it in the Russian Revolution, whereas it played an enormous part in the French Revolution. In that respect, Lenin, with his coarseness, his lack of any sort of embellishment or theatricality, with his simplicity merging into cynicism, was a typical Russian. Around those figures of majesty and glory, Peter the Great and Napoleon, the Russian people created a legend that they were antichrists.

The bourgeois virtues are lacking among the Russians, precisely those virtues which are so highly valued in Western Europe; while the bourgeois vices are to be found among the Russians, just those vices which are recognized as such. The word 'bourgeois', both adjective and noun, was a term which expressed disapproval in Russia at the very time when in the West it indicated a social position which commanded respect. Contrary to the opinion of the Slavophils the Russian people are less family-minded than the peoples of the West; they are less shackled to the family and break with it with comparative ease. The authority of parents among the Intelligentsia, the gentry and the middle classes, with the exception perhaps of the merchant class, was weaker than in the West. Generally speaking the feeling for graduation of rank was comparatively weak among the Russians or it existed in the negative form of servility, that is to say as a vice and not as a virtue. In the deep manifestations of its spirit the Russian people is the least philistine of all peoples, the least determined by external forces, and the least fettered to limiting forms of life, the least disposed to value the forms of life. Given this fact, the most Russian manner of life, for instance, that of the merchant class, as described by Ostrovsky, became repulsive to a degree which was unknown to the people of Western civilization. But this bourgeois manner of life was not revered as sacred. In the Russian the nihilist readily comes to the surface. 'We are all nihilists,' says Dostoyevsky. Side by side with servility and selfishness, the rebel, the anarchist comes easily into view; everything flows on into extremes of opposition, and all the while there is a striving after something final. Among the Russians there is always a thirst for another life, another world; there is always discontent with that which is. An eschatological bent is native to the structure of the Russian soul. Pilgrimage is a very characteristic Russian thing, to a degree unknown in the West. A pilgrim walks about the immense Russian land but never settles down or attaches himself to anything. A pilgrim is in search of the truth, in search of the Kingdom of God. He struggles into the distance; the pilgrim has no abiding city upon earth, he moves eagerly towards the city that is to be. The masses of the people have always produced pilgrims from their ranks, but in spirit the most creative representatives of Russian culture were pilgrims; Gogol, Dostoyevsky, Tolstoy, Solovëv and the whole of the revolutionary Intelligentsia were pilgrims. Not only physical but spiritual pilgrimage exists; it is the impossibility of finding rest and peace in anything finite, it is the striving towards infinity. But this too is an eschatological striving which is waiting in the expectation that to everything finite there will come an end, that ultimate truths will be revealed, that in the future there will be something extraordinary. I should call this a messianic sensitiveness which belongs alike to men of the people and men of the highest culture. Russians are Chiliasts in a greater or less degree, consciously or unconsciously. Western people are much more settled, more attached to the perfected forms of their civilization; they assign a greater value to their present experience and pay more attention to the good order of earthly life; they are afraid of infinity as chaos, and in this respect they are like the ancient Greeks. The Russian word for 'elemental' is with difficulty translated into foreign languages; it is difficult to give a name when that to which it applies has itself become enfeebled and almost disappeared. But the elemental is the source, the past, the strength of life, while the spirit of eschatology is a turning to the future, to the end of things. In Russia these two threads are united.

2

It was my good fortune to come into personal contact with wandering Russia during approximately ten years of this century, with the Russia which is searching for God and divine truth. I can speak about this phenomenon which is so characteristic of Russia, not from books but as the outcome of personal impressions, and I can say that it is one of the most powerful impressions of my life. In Moscow, in a tavern near the church of Florus and Laurus there used to take place at one time popular religious discussions every Sunday. The tavern was at the time called Yama (The Pit). To these meetings, which acquired a popular tone if only from the admirable Russian which was spoken there, used to come representatives of the most varied sects. There were 'immortalists' and Baptists and Tolstoyans and Evangelists of various shades, and *khlysty* who commonly kept themselves hidden and a few individuals who were theosophists from among the people. I used to go to these meetings and take an active part in the discussions. I was struck by the earnestness of the spiritual quest, the grip upon some one idea or other, the search for the truth about life and sometimes by a profoundly thought-out theory. The sectarian was always inclined to show a restrictedness of thought, a lack of universalism and a failure to recognize the complex manifoldness of life. But what a reproach to official Orthodoxy those ordinary people seeking after God were. The Orthodox missioner who was present was a pitiable figure and gave the impression of being a police functionary. Those people in search of divine truth wanted Christianity to be given actual effect to in life; they wanted more spirituality in relation to life; they would not acquiesce in its adaptation to the laws of this world. A particular interest was provided by the mystical sect of the immortalists who assert that he who believes in Christ will never die and that people die simply because they believe in death and do not believe in the victory of Christ over death. I talked to the immortalists a great deal;

198

they found me approachable and I am convinced that it is impossible to change their convictions; they were defending a certain part of the truth, not taking it in its fullness but partially. Some of these simple folk had their share of divine wisdom and were in possession of a whole gnostic system which reminded one of Jacob Boehme and other mystics of the gnostic type. The dualist element was usually strong and the difficulty of solving the problem of evil was a torment. But, as is not infrequently the case, the dualism was paradoxically combined with monism. In the government of N., next to an estate where I spent the summer every year, there was a colony founded by a Tolstovan, a very remarkable man. To this colony there flocked seekers after God and divine truth from all quarters of Russia. Sometimes they spent a few days in this colony and went on further into the Caucasus. All those who came used to call on me and we had conversations on spiritual matters, which were sometimes of extraordinary interest. There were many *Dobrolyubovsti*. These were followers of Alexander Dobrolyubov, a 'decadent' poet who went to the people, adopted the simple life and became a teacher of the spiritual life. Any contact with the *Dobrolyubovsti* was difficult because they had a vow of silence. All these seekers after God had their system of salvation for the world and were heart and soul devoted to it. They all considered this world in which they happened to be living as evil and godless and they were in search of another world, another life. In their attitude to this world, to history, to contemporary civilization, their frame of mind was eschatological. This world is coming to an end and a new world is beginning with them. Their thirst for spiritual things was intense and its presence among the Russian people was highly characteristic. They were Russian pilgrims. I remember a simple peasant, an ordinary labourer, still very young, and the conversation that I had with him. I found it easier to talk on spiritual and mystical subjects with him than with cultured people of the Intelligentsia. He described a mystical experience which he had passed through, which reminded me very much of what Eckhardt and Boehme wrote, writers about whom he, of course, had no knowledge whatever. The birth of God out of the darkness had been revealed to him. I cannot imagine Russia and the Russian people without these seekers

199

after divine truth. In Russia there has always been and there always will be spiritual pilgrimage; there has always been this striving after a final order of things. Among the Russian revolutionary Intelligentsia who professed in the majority of cases the most pitiable materialistic ideology, it would seem there could be no eschatology. But they think as they do because they ascribe too exclusive an importance to intellectual ideas which in many cases merely touch the surface of a man. At a deeper level, one which had not found expression in conscious thought, in Russian nihilism and socialism, there did exist an eschatological mentality; there was eschatological tension; there was an orientation towards the end. The talk always turned upon some final perfect state of existence which ought to arrive and take the place of the evil unjust and slavish world. 'Shigalev looked as though he was waiting for the destruction of the world, just as though it was coming the day after tomorrow morning, at exactly 25 minutes past 10.' Here Dostoyevsky divines something most essential in the Russian revolutionary. Russian revolutionaries, anarchists and socialists were unconscious Chiliasts; they expected the thousand years' reign. The revolutionary myth is a Chiliastic myth. The Russian nature is particularly favourable to the reception of it. It is a Russian idea that individual salvation is impossible, that salvation is corporate, that all are answerable for all. Dostoyevsky's attitude to the Russian revolutionary socialists was complex and two-sided. On the one hand he wrote against it in a way which almost amounted to lampooning, but on the other hand he said that those who revolted against Christianity are all the same Christlike people.

3

It might be thought that there is no eschatology in Tolstoy, that his religious philosophy being monistic and Indian in its affinities takes no cognizance of the problem of the end of the world. But such a judgment would be only superficial. Tolstoy's withdrawal from his family in the face of death is an eschatological withdrawal and full of profound meaning. He was a spiritual pilgrim; throughout his life he had wished to become one but in this he was not successful. But the pilgrim is bent upon the end; he wants to find himself an outlet from history, from civilization, into the natural divine life; and this is a striving towards the end, towards the thousand years' reign. Tolstoy was not an evolutionist who would wish for a gradual movement of history towards the longed-for end, towards the Kingdom of God; he was a maximalist and desired a break with history; he wanted to see the end of history. He does not wish to go on living in history, which rests upon the godless law of the world; he wants to live in nature, and he confuses fallen nature which is subject to the evil laws of the world no less than history is, with nature which is transfigured and illuminated, nature which is divine. But the eschatological striving of Tolstoy is not open to doubt; he was in search of the perfect life. It was precisely because of his search for the perfect life and his exposure of the life which is vile and sinful that the Black Hundred even called for the murder of Tolstoy. This festering sore upon the Russian nation, which dared to call itself the Union of the Russian people, hated everything which is great in the Russians, everything creative, everything which witnessed to the high calling of the Russian people in the world. The extreme orthodox hate and reject Tolstoy on account of the fact that he was excommunicated by the Holy Synod. The great question is, could the Synod be recognized as an organ of the Church of Christ and was it not rather typical of the kingdom of Caesar. To repudiate Leo Tolstoy means to repudiate the Russian genius. In the last resort it means the repudiation of the Russian vocation in the world. To set a high value upon Tolstoy in the history of the Russian idea certainly does not mean the acceptance of his religious philosophy, which I regard as weak and unacceptable from the point of view of Christian thought. One's appraisal of him must be based rather upon his personality as a whole, upon the path he chose, upon his quest, upon his criticism of the evil reality of history and of the sins of historical Christianity, and upon his ardent craving for the perfect life. Tolstoy put himself in touch with the spiritual movement among the masses of the people, of which I have spoken, and in this respect he is unique among Russian writers. Together with Dostoyevsky who was so entirely unlike him, he represents the Russian genius at its highest. Tolstoy, who all his life was a penitent said these proud words of himself: 'I am the sort of person I am, and what sort of person I am I know and God knows.' But it behoves us also to get to know the sort of person he was.

The creative work of Dostoyevsky is eschatological through and through. It is interested only in the ultimate, only in what is orientated to the end. The prophetic element is more powerful in Dostoyevsky than in any other Russian writer. His prophetic art consists in the fact that he revealed the volcanic ground of the spirit; he described the inner revolution of the spirit. He drew attention to inward catastrophe, from which new souls take their beginning. Together with Nietzsche and Kierkegaard he is a revealer of the tragic in the nineteenth century. There is a fourth dimension in man. It is shown by his orientation towards the ultimate, by his getting away from the intervening existence, from the universally obligatory, to which the name of 'allness' has been given. It is precisely in Dostoyevsky that the Russian messianic consciousness makes itself most keenly felt, much more so than in the Slavophils. It is to him that the words 'The Russian people is a God-bearing people' belong. These words are put into the mouth of Shatov. But in the figure of Shatov there is also revealed the twofold nature of the messianic consciousness, a twofoldness which existed already among the Hebrew people. Shatov began to believe that the Russian people is a God-bearing people when already he no longer believed in God. For him the Russian people became God; he was an idolator. Dostoyevsky exposes this with great power, but the impression remains that there is something of Shatov's point of view in Dostoyevsky himself. In any case he did believe in the great God-bearing mission of the Russian people; he believed that the Russians as a people were bound to say their own word to the world, a new word, at the end of time. The idea of a final perfected condition of mankind, of an earthly paradise, played an immense part in Dostoyevsky, and he displays a complex dialectic which is connected with this idea. It is always that same dialectic of freedom. *The Dream of the Ridiculous Man* and Versilov's dream in *The Youngster* are devoted to this idea. It is one from which Dostoyevsky's thought could never free itself. He understood perfectly well that the messianic consciousness is universal and he spoke about the universal vocation of the people. Messianism has nothing in common with an exclusive nationalism. Messianism opens out, it does not shut off. For this reason, in his speech on Pushkin, Dostoyevsky says that the Russian is the All-man, that there is in him a sensitiveness which answers the call of all men. The vocation of the Russian people is seen in an eschatological perspective and because of that, this thought of his presents a contrast with that of the idealists of the 'thirties and 'forties. Dostoyevsky's eschatological view is expressed in his prediction of the appearance of the Man-God. The figure of Kirillov is in this respect particularly important. In him Nietzsche and the idea of the superman is heralded. He who conquers pain and fear will be God. Time 'will be extinct in the mind'; 'that man will put an end to the world' to whom the name 'Man-God' will be given. The atmosphere of the conversation between Kirillov and Stavrogin is absolutely eschatological. The conversation was about the end of time. Dostoyevsky wrote not about the present but about the future. *The Possessed* was written about the future. It was about our own day rather than about the time in which it was written. Dostoyevsky's prophecy about the Russian Revolution is a penetrating view into the depth of the dialectic of man, of man who reaches out beyond the frontiers of average normal consciousness. It is characteristic that the negative side of the prophecy has shown itself to be more true than the positive. The political predictions were altogether weak. But of greater interest than all else is the fact that the very Christianity of Dostoyevsky was directed towards the future, towards a new crowning epoch in Christianity. Dostoyevsky's prophetic spirit led him beyond the bounds of historical Christianity. The *Starets* Zosima was the prophecy of a new *starchestvo*; he was entirely different from the *Starets* Ambrose of Optina, and the *Startsi* of Optina did not recognize him as one of themselves.[1] Alësha Karamazov was the prophecy of a new type of Christian and he bore little resemblance to the usual Orthodox type. But the *Starets* Zosima and Alësha Karamazov were less successful than Ivan Karamazov and Dmitri Karamazov. This is explained by the difficulty which prophetic art found in creating the characters. But K. Leontyev was right when he said that

[1] The figure of St Tikhon of Zadonsky who was a Christian humanist of the eighteenth century had a very great influence upon Dostoyevsky.

Dostoyevsky's Orthodoxy was not traditional Orthodoxy, that his was not Byzantine monastic Orthodoxy, but a new Orthodoxy into which humanitarianism entered. But it must by no means be said that it was rose-coloured; it was tragic. He thought that rebellion against God might occur in man because of the divine element in him; it might arise from his feeling for righteousness and pity, and from the sense of his own value and dignity. Dostoyevsky preached a Johannine Christianity, the Christianity of a transfigured earth, and above all a religion of resurrection. The traditional *starets* would not have said what the *Starets* Zosima says: 'Brothers, do not be afraid of the sin of man, love man even in his sin: love all God's creation, both the whole and every speck of it; love every leaf, love every ray of God, love the animals, love the plants, love every single thing; we will love every single thing and arrive at the divine mystery in things.' 'Kiss the earth, and unceasingly, insatiably love. Love all men; seek out the triumph and the ecstasy of it!' In Dostoyevsky there were the beginnings of a new Christian anthropology and cosmology; there was a new orientation to the created world, one which was strange to patristic Orthodoxy. Marks of similarity might be found in the West in Saint Francis of Assisi. It shows a transition already from historical Christianity to eschatological Christianity.

Towards the end of the nineteenth century there developed in Russia an apocalyptic frame of mind which was connected with a sense of the approach of the end of the world and the appearance of antichrist, that is to say it was tinged with pessimism. They were expecting not so much a new Christian era and the coming of the Kingdom of God as the coming of the kingdom of antichrist. It was a profound disillusionment about the ways of history and a disbelief in the continued existence of historical problems. It was a break with the Russian idea. Some are disposed to explain this expectation of the end of the world by a presentiment of the end of the Russian Empire, of the Russian realm, which was considered sacred. The principal writers who expressed this apocalyptic frame of mind were K. Leontyev and Vladimir Solovëv. Leontyev's apocalyptic pessimism had two sources. His philosophy of history and his sociology, which was grounded in biology, taught the inevitable approach of the decrepitude of all societies, states and civilizations.

He connected this decrepitude with liberal egalitarian progress. Decrepitude to him meant also ugliness, the ruin of beauty which belonged to the flower of culture of the past. This sociological theory which laid claim to be scientific, was with him combined with a religious apocalyptic trend of thought. Loss of belief in the possibility that Russia could still produce an original flourishing culture of its own, had an immense importance in the growth of this gloomy apocalyptic state of mind. He always thought that everything on earth was precarious and untrustworthy. Leontyev gave too much of a naturalistic turn to his conception of the end of the world; with him spirit is at no time and in no place active; for him there is no freedom. He never believed in the Russian people and certainly did not expect anything original to be produced by the Russian people, that could only come from the Byzantinism which was imposed upon them from above. But the time came when this mistrust of the Russian people became acute and hopeless. He makes this terrible prediction: 'Russian society which even apart from that was egalitarian enough in its customs, is rushing still more swiftly than any other society along the deadly path of universal confusion, and from the womb of our State, which is first of all classless and then Churchless, or at least with but a feeble' Church, we shall unexpectedly give birth to antichrist.' The Russian people is not capable of anything else. Leontyev foresaw the Russian Revolution and divined many of its characteristics; he foresaw that the Revolution would not be made with gloved hands, that there would be no freedom in it, that freedom will be entirely taken away, and that the age-long instincts of obedience will be required for the Revolution. The Revolution will be socialistic but not liberal and not democratic; the defenders of freedom will be swept away. While predicting a horrible and cruel revolution Leontyev at the same time recognized that the problem of the relations between labour and capital must be solved; he was a reactionary but he acknowledged the hopelessness of reactionary principles, and the inevitability of revolution. He foresaw not only a Russian but also a world revolution. This presentiment of the inevitability of world revolution takes an apocalyptic form and is represented as the coming of the end of the world. 'Antichrist is coming', exclaims Leontyev. In his case the interpretation of the Apocalypse was entirely passive. Man can do nothing at all, he can only save his own soul. This apocalyptic pessimism attracted Leontyev aesthetically; he enjoyed the idea that right would not triumph on earth. He did not share the Russian craving for universal salvation; and any sort of striving after the transfiguration of mankind and of the world was quite lacking in him. The idea of *sobornost* and the idea of theocracy were essentially foreign to him; he accused Dostoyevsky and Tolstoy of taking a rosy view of Christianity and of humanitarianism. The eschatological views of Leontyev are of a negative kind and not in the least characteristic of the Russian eschatological idea. But it cannot be denied that he was an acute and forthright thinker and that he frequently showed perspicacity in his view of history.

Solovëv's cast of mind changed very much towards the end of his life; it becomes gloomily apocalyptic. He writes *Three Conversations* which contains a veiled controversy with Tolstoy, and to this is added *A Story about Antichrist*. He becomes finally disillusioned about his own theocratic utopia; he no longer believes in humanist progress; he does not believe in his own fundamental idea of God-manhood, or rather his idea of God-manhood becomes terribly restricted. A pessimistic view of the end of history took possession of him and he feels that that end is imminent. In *A Story about Antichrist* Solovëv above all else squares accounts with his own personal past, with his theocratic humanitarian illusions. It represents above all the collapse of his theocratic utopia; he believes no more in the possibility of a Christian State, and his loss of belief is very advantageous, both to himself and to everyone else. But he goes further; he does not believe in historical problems in general. History is coming to an end and super-history is beginning. The union of the Churches which he continued to desire, will take place beyond the frontiers of history. In regard to his theocratic ideas Solovëv belongs to the past; he rejects this outlived past, but he becomes of a pessimistic and apocalyptic frame of mind. A contradiction exists between the theocratic idea and eschatology. Theocracy realized in history, excludes the eschatological outlook; it makes the end, as it were, immanent in history itself. The Church, understood as a kingdom, the Christian State, and Christian civilization take the vigour out of the search for the Kingdom of God. In Solověv's earlier period his sense of evil had been lacking in strength; now the sense of evil becomes predominant. He set himself a very difficult task in drawing the figure of antichrist; he did this not in a theological and philosophical form but in the form of a story. It was possible to carry this through apparently only by adopting a jocular tone, a form in which he was so fond of taking refuge when the matter under discussion was something very secret and intimate. It shocked a great many people, but this jocularity may be understood as shyness. I do not share the opinion of those who place *A Story about Antichrist* almost higher than anything of Solověv's. It is very interesting, and without it it is impossible to understand the path along which Solověv moved. But the story belongs to inaccurate and out-of-date interpretations of the Apocalypse, the sort in which too much is assigned to time at the expense of eternity. It is passive, not active and not creative eschatology; there is no expectation of a new era of the Holy Spirit. In his drawing of the figure of antichrist it is a mistake that he is depicted as a lover of men, as a humanitarian who makes social righteousness an effective reality. This, so to speak, justified the most revolutionary and obscurantist apocalyptic theories. In actual fact if we are talking about antichrist it is truer to say that he will be absolutely inhuman and will be responsible for a stage of extreme dehumanization. Dostoyevsky was more in the right when he describes the spirit of antichrist as above all hostile to freedom and contemptuous of man. *The Legend of the Grand Inquisitor* stands on a higher level than *A Story about Antichrist*. The English Roman Catholic writer, Benson, wrote a novel which is very reminiscent of *A Story about Antichrist*. All this takes a line which moves in the opposite direction to that of an active creative interpretation of the end of the world. The teaching of Solověv about God-manhood, if it is finally worked out, ought to result in an active, not a passive, eschatology; it ought to lead to the thought of the creative vocation of man at the end of history, a creative vocation which alone makes possible the coming of the end of the world, and the Second Advent of Christ. The end of history, the end of the world, is a divine-human end; it depends upon man also and upon human activity. In Solověv it is not clear what is the positive result of the divine-human process in history. In his earlier period he mistakenly regarded it too much as a matter of evolution. Now he truly regards the end of history as catastrophic. But the idea of catastrophe does not mean that there will be no positive result of the creative work of man on behalf of the Kingdom of God. The one positive thing in Solovëv is the union of the Churches in the persons of Pope Peter, *Starets* Ioann and Dr. Paulus. Orthodoxy appears as in the main mystical. Solovëv's eschatology is nevertheless above all an eschatology of judgment. That is one of the aspects of eschatology, but there ought to be another. The attitude of N. Fedorov to the Apocalypse is entirely different.

Fedorov was little known and valued in his lifetime. It was our generation at the beginning of the twentieth century which became specially interested in him.[1] He was just an ordinary librarian at the Rumyantsev Museum and he lived on 17 roubles a month. He was an ascetic and slept on a chest, and at the same time he was an opponent of the ascetic interpretation of Christianity. Fedorov was a typical Russian, a native genius, an original. He published next to nothing during his lifetime. After his death his friends published his *Philosophy of the Common Task* in two volumes, which they distributed gratis to a small circle of people, since Fedorov considered the sale of books was not to be tolerated. He was a Russian searcher after universal salvation; in him the sense of the responsibility of all for all reached its ultimate and most trenchant expression. Each person is answerable for the whole world and for all men, and every person is bound to strive for the salvation of all men and of everything. Western people are easily reconciled to the idea of the perishing of the many; this is probably due to the part which righteousness plays in Western thought. N. Fedorov was not a writer by nature; the only thing he wrote is this 'project' of universal salvation. At times he reminds one of such people as Fourier; there is a combination of fantasy and practical realism in him, of mysticism and rationalism, of day-dreaming and sobriety. But here is what some of the most notable of Russians have said about him. Vladimir Solovëv writes of him 'Your "project" I accept unreservedly and without any

[1] One of the first essays on N. Fedorov was my own, 'The Religion of the Resurrection' in *Russian Thought*.

discussion. Since the time of the appearance of Christianity your "project" is the first forward movement of the human spirit along the way of Christ. For my part I can only regard you as my teacher and spiritual father.'[1] Tolstoy says of Fedorov: 'I am proud to be living at the same time as such a man.' Dostoyevsky too held a very high opinion of Fedorov and wrote of him: 'He (Fedorov) aroused my interest more than enough. I am essentially in complete agreement with these ideas, I have accepted them, so to speak, as my own.' What then is to be said of Fedorov's 'project' and of the extraordinary thoughts which Russians of the greatest genius found so striking? Fedorov was the only man whose life profoundly impressed Tolstoy. At the basis of his whole outlook on life was the compassion Fedorov felt for the sorrows of men; and there was no man on earth who felt such grief at human death and such a craving for their return to life. He regarded sons as to blame for the death of their fathers; he called sons 'prodigal sons' because they forgot the tombs of their fathers; they were lured away from them by their wives, by capitalism and civilization; civilization was built upon the bones of the fathers. Fedorov's general view of life was as regards its sources akin to slavophilism; there is to be found in him the idealization of the patriarchal structure of society, of the patriarchal monarchy, and hostility to Western culture. But he goes beyond the limits of the Slavophils, and there are entirely revolutionary elements in him, such as the activity of man, collectivism, the determining importance of labour, his ideas of economic management, and the high value he places upon positive science and technical knowledge. During the Soviet period in Russia there have been tendencies which sprang from the followers of Fedorov. And however strange it may be there was a certain contact between the teaching of Fedorov and communism in spite of his very hostile attitude to Marxism. But Fedorov's hostility to capitalism was still greater than that of the Marxists. His chief idea, his 'project' is concerned with the control of the elemental forces of nature, with the subjection of nature to man. With him belief in the might of man goes further than Marxism and it is more audacious. What is absolutely original in him is his com-

[1] See V. A. Kozhevnikov's book, *Nicolai Fedorovitch Fedorov* which is very rich in material.

bination of the Christian faith with belief in the power of science and technical knowledge; he believed that a return to life for all the dead, an active revivifying and not merely a passive waiting for the resurrection, ought to be not only a Christian task, Divine service outside the Church, but also an undertaking which is positively scientific and technical. There are two sides to the teaching of Fedorov, his interpretation of the Apocalypse—an effort of genius and unique in the history of Christianity, and his 'project' of the resuscitation of the dead, in which there is, of course, a fantastic element. But his moral thought is at its height the very loftiest in the history of Christianity.

There was great breadth of knowledge in Fedorov, but his culture belonged rather to natural science than to philosophy. He had a great dislike of philosophical idealism and so he had of the gnostic tendencies which were to be found in Solovëv. He was a man of a single idea; he was entirely in the grip of one notion, that of victory over death, of the return of the dead to life. And both in his appearance and in the form of his thought there was something austere. The remembrance of death, in connection with which there exists a Christian prayer, was always present with him. He lived and thought in the face of death, not his own death but that of other people, the death of all men who had died throughout history. But the sternness in him, which would not consent to the use of any destructive force, was an outcome of his optimistic belief in the possibility of the final conquest of death, in the possibility not only of resurrection but also of resuscitation, that is to say, of an active part taken by man in the task of the universal renewal of life. Fedorov is to be credited with a completely original exposition of the apocalyptic prophecies, one which may be called active as distinct from the passive interpretation which is usual. He proposed to interpret the apocalyptic prophecy as dependent on certain conditions, a line which had never been taken hitherto; and in fact it is impossible to understand the end of the world with which the prophecies of the Apocalypse are concerned as a fated destiny. That would be to contradict the Christian idea of freedom. The fated end described in the Apocalypse comes as the result of following the path of evil. If the commandments of Christ are not fulfilled by men, such and such a thing will be inevitable, but if Christian mankind is united for the common fraternal task of the conquest of death and the achievement of universal resurrection, it can escape the fatal end of the world, the appearance of antichrist, the last judgment and hell. Mankind can in that case pass over directly into eternal life. The Apocalypse is a threat to mankind, steeped as it is in evil, and it faces man with an active problem; a merely passive waiting for the terrible end is unworthy of man. Fedorov's eschatology is sharply distinguished from that of Solovëv and Leontyev, and the right is on his side, the future belongs to him. He is a decided enemy of the traditional understanding of immortality and resurrection. 'The Last Judgment is only a threat to mankind in its infancy. The covenant of Christianity consists in the union of the heavenly and the earthly, of the divine and the human; while the universal resuscitation is an immanent resuscitation achieved by the whole heart, by every thought, every act, that is, by all the powers and capacities of all the sons of men; and it is the fulfilment of the law of Christ, the Son of God and at the same time the Son of Man.' Resuscitation stands in opposition to progress, which comes to terms with the death of every generation. Resuscitation is a reversal of time, it is an activity of man in relation to the past and not to the future only. Resuscitation is also opposed to civilization and culture which flourish in cemeteries and are founded upon forgetfulness of the death of our fathers. Fedorov regarded capitalist civilization as a great evil; he is an enemy of individualism and a supporter of religious and social collectivism, of the brotherhood of man. The common Christian task ought to begin in Russia as the country which is least corrupted by godless civilization. Fedorov professed Russian messianism. But in what did this mysterious project' consist, which struck men so, and aroused the enthusiasm of some and the mockery of others? It is nothing more nor less than a 'project' to escape the Last Judgment. The victory over death, the universal resuscitation is not just an act of God in regard to which man remains passive; it is the work of God-manhood, that is, it is also the work of collective human activity. It must be admitted that in Fedorov's 'project' the perspicacity of genius in his exposition of the apocalyptic prophecies, and the extraordinary loftiness of moral thought in the conception of the common responsibility of all for all, are combined with utopian fantasy. The author of the 'project' believes that science and technical knowledge can become capable of reanimating the dead and that man can finally master the elemental forces of nature, that he can control nature and subordinate it to himself. And, of course, he brings this all the while into union with the resuscitating power of religion, with belief in the Resurrection of Christ. But nevertheless he rationalizes the mystery of death. He has an inadequate sense of the significance of the Cross; to him Christianity was simply a religion of resurrection. He had no feeling at all for the irrationality of evil. In Fedorov's teaching there is a very great deal which ought to be retained, as entering into the Russian Idea. I do not know a more characteristically Russian thinker. He is one who must appear strange to the West. He desires the brotherhood of man not only in space but also in time, and he believes in the possibility of changing the past. But the materialist methods of resuscitation which he proposes cannot be retained. The problem of the relation of the spirit to the natural world he did not think out to its final end.

Messianism is a characteristic not only of the Russians but also of the Poles. Poland's destiny of suffering has made it more acute in its own case. It is interesting to place Russian messianic and eschatological ideas side by side with those of the greatest philosopher of Polish messianism, Cieszkowski, who has not hitherto been sufficiently appreciated. His principal writing, the four-volume work *Notre Père* is constructed in the form of an exposition of The Lord's Prayer.[1] It is an original exposition of Christianity as a whole, but in particular it is a Christian philosophy of history. Like the Slavophils and Vladimir Solověv, Cieszkowski passed through German idealism and came under the influence of Hegel, but his thought remained independent and creative. He wants to remain a Roman Catholic; he does not break with the Roman Catholic Church, but he passes over the frontiers of historical Catholicism. He gives expression to a religion of the Holy Spirit more definitely than the Russian thinkers. He is bent upon what he calls *Révélation de la Révélation*. The full revelation of God is a revelation of the Holy Spirit. God even is the Holy Spirit; that is His real Name. Spirit

[1] Published in French, Cte A. Cieszkowskie, *Notre Père*, 4 volumes.

212

is the highest entity; everything is Spirit and through Spirit. It is only in the third revelation of the Spirit, complete and synthetic, that the Holy Trinity is disclosed. The dogma of the Trinity could not yet be revealed in Holy Scripture. Only silence on the subject of the Holy Spirit was in his view orthodox; everything else was to be regarded as heretical, the Persons of the Holy Trinity, their names, their natures and the moments of their revelation. Those who are very orthodox will probably find in Cieszkowski a tendency to Sabellianism. In Cieszkowski's opinion there was a partial truth in the heresies, but not the full truth; he predicted the coming of the new era of the Holy Spirit. It is only the era of the Paraclete which will provide a full revelation. Following German idealism he affirmed, as did Solovëv, spiritual progress, spiritual development. Mankind could not yet take the Holy Spirit to itself; it was not yet sufficiently mature. But the time of the special activity of the Holy Spirit is drawing near; the spiritual maturity of man will come when he has it within his power to take the revelation of the Holy Spirit into himself and to profess a religion of the Spirit. The operation of the Spirit spreads through all mankind. The Spirit will embrace both soul and body. Into the era of the Spirit social and cultural elements of human progress will also enter. Cieszkowski lays stress upon the social spirit of Slavdom; he looks for the revelation of the Word in social act. In this he displays a similarity to Russian thought. He preaches *Communauté du St Esprit*. Mankind will live in the name of the Paraclete; the Our Father is a prophetic prayer. The Church is not yet the Kingdom of God. Man takes an active part in the creation of the new world. A very interesting idea of Cieszkowski's is that the world acts upon God. The establishment of social harmony among men which will be conformable to the era of the Holy Spirit, will lead to absolute harmony within the Godhead. The suffering of God is a mark of His holiness. Cieszkowski had been a follower of Hegel and, therefore, recognizes dialectic development. The advent of the new era of the Holy Spirit which will embrace the whole social life of mankind, he views in the aspect of development rather than in the aspect of catastrophe. There cannot be a new religion but there can be a creative development of the eternal religion. The religion of the Holy Spirit is also the eternal Christian religion. To

Cieszkowski belief is knowledge which is accepted by feeling. He has a great many interesting philosophical ideas which I cannot stay to dwell upon here. Cieszkowski's teaching is not so much about the end of the world as about the end of an age, about the coming of a new æon. Time is to him part of eternity. Cieszkowski was, of course, a great optimist; he was filled with hope of the speedy coming of the new æon, although there was little that was consoling in his environment. This optimism was proper to the period in which he lived. We cannot be so optimistic, but this does not prevent us from appreciating the importance of his fundamental ideas. Much of his thought is similar to Russian thought, to the Christian hopes of the Russians. Cieszkowski was entirely unknown among us, no-one ever quotes or refers to him, just as he also knew nothing of Russian thought. The similarity is apparently one which is due to the nature of Slav thought in general. In certain respects I am prepared to place the thought of Cieszkowski higher than Solo-věv's, although the personality of the latter was more complex and richer, and it contained more inconsistencies. The similarity lay in the opinion they shared that there must come a new era in Christianity, which will be the eve of a new outpouring of the Holy Spirit, and that man will take an active, not merely a passive part in this. The apocalyptic cast of mind awaits the fulfilment of revelation. The Church of the New Testament is only a symbolical figure of the eternal Church.

Three notable Russian thinkers, Vladimir Solověv, N. Fedorov and V. Rozanov, gave expression to some very profound ideas on the subject of death and on the relation which exists between death and birth. Their thoughts are varied and even contradictory. But what interested all of them more than anything else was the victory of eternal life over death. Solověv postulates a contradiction between the view which dwells upon the prospect of eternal life for the individual person, and that which envisages the family in which the birth of a new life leads on to the death of the preceding generations. The meaning of love lies in victory over death and the attainment of eternal individual life. Fedorov too sees the connection between birth and death; sons are born, and forget the death of their fathers.

But victory over death points to a demand for the resuscitation of the fathers, a transmutation of the energy which gives birth into the energy which resuscitates. In contrast to Solovëv, Fedorov is not a philosopher of *Eros*. In Rozanov we have a third point of view. I shall speak about this extraordinary writer in the following chapter. At the moment I will speak only of his solution of the question of death and birth. All Rozanov's creativeness is an apotheosis of birth-giving life. In the generative process which continually gives birth to new life after new life, Solovëv and Fedorov see an element of death and the poisoning pollution of sin. Rozanov, on the contrary, wants to deify generative sex. Birth is even a triumph over death; it is the eternal blooming of life. Sex is holy because it is the source of life; it is the contrary of death. Such a solution of the question is connected with a deficient feeling for and awareness of personality. The birth of an innumerable quantity of new generations cannot reconcile us to the death of one single man. In any case Russian thought had reflected profoundly upon the theme of death, of victory over death, and upon birth and the metaphysics of sex. All three thinkers grasped the fact that the subject of death and birth is one which concerns the metaphysical depth of sex. In Vladimir Solovëv the energy of sex in eros-love ceases to be generative and leads to personal immortality; he is a platonist. In Fedorov the energy of sex is turned into the energy which revivifies dead fathers. In Rozanov, who returns to Judaism and paganism, the energy of sex is sanctified as being that which generates a new life, and in so doing conquers death. It is a very notable fact that in Russian religion it is the Resurrection which is of chief importance. This is an essential difference from the religion of the West in which the Resurrection recedes to a second place. For Roman Catholic and Protestant thought the problem of sex was exclusively a social and moral problem; it was not a metaphysical and cosmic problem as it was to Russian thought. This is explained by the fact that the West has been too exclusively occupied with civilization, too much socialized; its Christianity was too academic. The mystery of the Resurrection itself has not been a cosmic mystery, but a dogma which has lost its living significance. The mystery of cosmic life has been concealed by the organized forms of social life. There was, of course, Jacob

215

Boehme who did not fall a prey to this spirit of social organization. It is indisputable that, taken as a whole, Western thought is of great importance to the solution of the problem of religious anthropology and religious cosmology. But Roman Catholic and Protestant thought in their official form are very little concerned with these problems in their full depth, as distinct from questions of ecclesiastical organization and academic guidance. In Orthodoxy there was no organically-absorbed Greco-Roman humanism; ascetic self-denial was predominant, but for precisely that reason upon the basis of Orthodoxy something new about man and the cosmos could more easily be revealed. Orthodoxy also did not adopt that active attitude towards history which Western Christianity displayed, but it may be just for that reason that it will show a distinctive attitude of its own towards the end of history. In Russian Orthodox religion there has always been hidden eschatological expectation.

There are three currents of thought which may be distinguished in Russian Orthodoxy and they may be found intertwined: the traditional monastic ascetic element which is connected with the *Dobrotolubie*; the cosmocentric current which perceives the divine energies in the created world, which devotes its attention to the transfiguration of the world, and with which sociology is connected; and the anthropocentric, historiosophic, eschatological current which is concerned with the activity of man in nature and society. The first of these currents of thought presents no creative problems at all, and in the past it has found its support not so much in Greek patristics as in Syrian ascetic literature. The second and third present problems concerned with the cosmos and with man. But behind all these distinguishable currents lies hidden the common Russian Orthodox religious sense which has worked out the type of Russian man, with his discontent with this world, with his gentleness of soul, with his dislike of the might of this world and with his struggle towards the other world, towards the end, towards the Kingdom of God. The soul of the Russian people has been nourished not so much upon sermons and doctrinal teaching as upon liturgical worship and the tradition of Christian kindliness which has penetrated into the very depth of the soul's structure. The Russians have thought that Russia is a country which is absolutely special and peculiar, with its own special vocation. But the principal thing was not Russia itself but that which Russia brings to the world, above all the brotherhood of man and freedom of the spirit. It is here that we come upon the most difficult question of all. The Russians are not striving for a kingdom which is of this world; they are not moved by the will to power and might. In their spiritual structure the Russians are not an imperialist people; they do not like the State. In this the Slavophils were right. But at the same time they are a colonizing people; they have a gift for colonization, and they have created the greatest State in the world. What does this mean? How is it to be understood? Enough has already been said about the dualistic structure of Russian history. The fact that Russia is so enormous is not only the good fortune and the blessing of the Russian people in history, but it is also the source of the tragic element in the fate of the Russian people. It was necessary to accept responsibility for the immensity of the Russian land and to bear the burden of it. The elemental immensity of the Russian land protected the Russian, but he himself was obliged to protect and organize the Russian land. The unhealthy hypertrophy of the State was accepted and it crushed the people and often tortured them. A substitution took place within the consciousness of the Russian idea, and of the Russian vocation. Both Moscow the Third Rome and Moscow the Third International were connected with the Russian messianic idea; they represented a distorted form of it. Never in history, I think, has there been a people which has combined such opposites in its history. Imperialism was always a distortion of the Russian idea and of the Russian vocation. But it was not by chance that Russia was so enormous. This immensity was providential and it is connected with the idea and the calling of the Russian people. The immensity of Russia is a metaphysical property of it, and does not only belong to its empirical history. The great Russian spiritual culture can only belong to an enormous country and an immense people. The great Russian literature could arise only among a very numerous people who live in an immense country. Russian literature and Russian thought were permeated by hatred of the Empire and they exposed the evil of it. But at the same time they presupposed an Empire, they presupposed the immensity of Russia. This contradiction is inherent in the very spiritual structure of Russia and the Russian people. The immensity of Russia might have been other than it was; it might not have been an Empire with all its evil aspects; it might have been a people's realm. But Russia took shape in grievous historical circumstances; the Russian land was surrounded by enemies; it was made use of by the evil forces of history.

The Russian Idea was recognized in various forms in the nineteenth century, but found itself in profound conflict with Russian history as it was built up by the forces which held sway in it. In this lies the tragic element in the historical destiny of Russia and also the complexity of our subject.

DEATH
AND
IMMORTALITY

Nicholas Berdyaev

Death and Immortality

ORDINARY systems of philosophical ethics do not deal with the problems of eschatology. If they treat of immortality, they do so without going deep into the question of death but discuss it chiefly in connection with man's moral responsibility, rewards and punishments, or, at best, with the need of satisfying his longing for infinity. The conception of immortality has been defended on the ground of a naturalistic metaphysics and the idea of the soul as a substance. It left completely untouched the problem of death, so fundamental for the religious and especially for the Christian consciousness. Death is a problem not only for metaphysics but also for ontological ethics. Thinkers like Kierkegaard and Heidegger recognize this. It also acquires a central significance in Freud. It is the problem of death, inseverably connected with that of time, that has a primary significance; the problem of immortality is secondary, and as a rule it has been wrongly formulated. The very word " immortality " is inexact and implies a rejection of the mysterious fact of death. The question of the immortality of the soul forms part of a metaphysic that is utterly out of date. Death is the most profound and significant fact of life, raising the least of mortals above the mean commonplaces of life. The fact of death alone gives true depth to the question as to the meaning of life. Life in this world has meaning just because there is death ; if there were no death in our world, life would be meaningless. The meaning is bound up with the end. If there were no end, i.e. if life in our world continued for ever, there would be no meaning in it. Meaning lies beyond the confines of this limited world,

317

and the discovery of meaning presupposes an end here. It is remarkable that although men rightly feel the horror of death and rightly regard it as the supreme evil, they are bound to connect with it the final discovery of meaning. Death—the supreme horror and evil—proves to be the only way out of the " bad time " into eternity ; immortal and eternal life prove to be only attainable through death. Man's last hope is connected with death, which manifests so clearly the power of evil in the world. This is the greatest paradox of death. According to the Christian religion death is the result of sin and is the last enemy, the supreme evil which must be conquered. And at the same time in our sinful world death is a blessing and a value. It inspires us with terror not merely because it is an evil, but because the depth and the greatness of it shatter our everyday world and exceed the powers accumulated by us in this life to meet this world's requirements. Spiritual enlightenment and an extraordinary intensity of spiritual life are needed to give us a right attitude towards death. Plato was right in teaching that philosophy was the practice of death. The only trouble is that philosophy as such does not know how one ought to die and how to conquer death. The philosophic doctrine of immortality does not show the way.

It might be said that ethics at its highest is concerned with death rather than with life, for death manifests the depth of life and reveals the end, which alone gives meaning to life. Life is noble only because it contains death, an end which testifies that man is destined to another and a higher life. Life would be low and meaningless if there were no death and no end.

Meaning is never revealed in an endless time ; it is to be found in eternity. But there is an abyss between life in time and life in eternity, and it can only be bridged by death and the horror of final severance. When this world apprehended as self-sufficient, completed and closed in, everything in it appears meaningless because everything is transitory and corruptible—i.e. death and mortality in this world is just what makes it meaningless. This is one-half of the truth seen from a narrow and limited point of view. Heidegger is right in saying that the herd-mentality (*das Man*) is insensitive to the anguish of death.[1] It feels merely a low fear of death as of that which makes life meaningless. But there is another half of the truth, concealed from the ordinary point of view. Death not merely makes life senseless and corruptible: it is also a sign, coming from the depths, of there being a higher meaning in life. Not base fear but horror and anguish which death inspires in us prove that we belong not only to the surface but to the depths as well, not only to temporal life but also to eternity. While we are in time, eternity both attracts and horrifies us. We feel horror and anguish not only because all that we hold dear dies and comes to an end, but still more because we are conscious of a yawning abyss between time and eternity. Horror and anguish at having to cross the abyss contain at the same time a hope that the final meaning shall be revealed and realized. Death holds hope as well as horror for man, though he does not always recognize this or call it by an appropriate name. The meaning that comes from the other world is like a scorching flame to us and demands that we should pass through death. Death is not only a biological and psychological fact but a spiritual fact as well. *The meaning of death is that there can be no eternity in time and that an endless temporal series would be meaningless.*

But death is a manifestation of life, it is found on this side of life and is life's reaction to its own demand for an end in time. Death cannot be understood merely as the last moment of life followed either by non-being or by existence in the world beyond. Death is an event embracing the whole of life. Our existence is full of death and dying. Life is perpetual dying, experiencing the end in everything, a continual judgment passed by eternity upon time. Life is a constant struggle against death and a partial dying of the human body and the human soul. Death within life is due to the impossibility of embracing the fullness of being, either in time or in space. Time and space are death-dealing, they give rise to disruptions which are a partial experience of death. When, in time, human

[1] See *Sein und Zeit*, chapter *Das mögliche Ganzsein des Daseins und das Sein zum Tode.*

feelings die and disappear, this is an experience of death. When, in space, we part with a person, a house, a town, a garden, an animal, and have the feeling that we may never see them again, this is an experience of death. The anguish of every parting, of every severance in time and space, is the experience of death. I remember what anguish I felt as a boy at every parting. It was so all-embracing that I lived through mortal anguish at the thought of never seeing again the face of a stranger I met, the town I happened to pass through, the room in which I spent a few days, a tree or a dog I saw. This was, of course, an experience of death within life.

Space and time cannot enfold the wholeness of being but condemn us to severances and separations, and death always triumphs in life ; it testifies that meaning is to be found in eternity and in fullness of being, that in the life in which meaning will triumph there shall be no parting, no dying, no corruption of human thoughts and feelings. We die not only in our own death but in the death of those we love. We have in life the experience of death, though not the final experience of it. And we cannot be reconciled to death— to the death neither of human beings nor of animals, plants, things or houses. The striving for eternity of all that exists is the essence of life. And yet eternity is reached only by passing through death, and death is the destiny of everything that exists in this world. The higher and more complex a being is, the more it is threatened with death. Mountains live longer than men, although their life is less complex and lower in quality ; Mont Blanc appears to be more immortal than a saint or a genius. Things are comparatively more stable than living beings.

Death has a positive significance, but at the same time it is the most terrible and the only evil. Every kind of evil in the last resort means death. Murder, hatred, malice, depravity, envy, vengeance are death and seeds of death. Death is at the bottom of every evil passion. Pride, greed, ambition are deadly in their results. There is no other evil in the world except death and killing. Death is the evil result of sin. A sinless life would be immortal and eternal. Death is a denial of eternity and therein lies its ontological evil, its hostility to existence, its striving to reduce creation to non-being. Death resists God's creation of the world and is a return to the original non-being. Death wants to free the creature by bringing it back to primeval freedom that preceded the creation of the world. There is but one way out for the creature which in its sin resists God's conception of it—death. Death is a negative testimony to God's power and to the Divine meaning manifested in the meaningless world. It might be said that the world would carry out its godless plan of an endless (but not eternal) life if there were no God ; but since God exists, that plan is not realizable and ends in death. The Son of God, the Redeemer and Saviour, absolutely sinless and holy, had to accept death, and thereby He sanctified death. Hence the double attitude of Christianity to death. Christ has destroyed death by His death. His voluntary death, due to the evil of the world, is a blessing and a supreme value. In worshipping the cross we worship death which gives us freedom and victory. In order to rise again we must die. Through the cross death is transfigured and leads us to resurrection and to life. The whole life of this world must be made to pass through death and crucifixion, else it cannot attain resurrection and eternity.

If death is accepted as a part of the mystery of life, it is not final and has not the last word. Rebellion against death in our world is rebellion against God. But at the same time we must wage a heroic struggle against death, conquer it as the last evil and pluck out its sting. The work of Christ in the world is in the first instance victory over death and preparation for resurrection and eternity. The good is life, power, fullness and eternity of life. Death proves to be the greatest paradox in the world, which cannot be understood rationally. Death is folly that has become commonplace. The consciousness that death is an ordinary everyday occurrence has dulled our sense of its being irrational and paradoxical. The last achievement of the rationalized herd-mind is to try to forget about death altogether, to conceal it, to bury the dead as unobtrusively as possible. It is the very opposite of the spirit expressed in the Christian prayer " ever to remember death ". In this respect modern civilized people are incomparably inferior to the ancient Egyptians.

The paradox of death takes an aesthetic as well as a moral form. Death is hideous, the acme of hideousness, it is dissolution, the loss of all image and form, the triumph of the lower elements of the material world. But at the same time death is beautiful, it ennobles the least of mortals and raises him to the level of the greatest, it overcomes the ugliness of the mean and the commonplace. There is a moment when the face of the dead is more beautiful and harmonious than it had been in life. Ugly, evil feelings pass away and disappear in the presence of death. Death, the greatest of evils, is more noble than life in this world. The beauty and charm of the past depends upon the ennobling influence of death. It is death that purifies the past and puts upon it the seal of eternity. Death brings with it not only dissolution but purification as well. Nothing perishable, spoiled and corruptible can stand the test of death—only the eternal can. Terrible as it is to admit it, the significance of life is bound up with death and is only revealed in the face of death. Man's moral worth is manifested in the test of death, which abounds in life itself.

But at the same time struggle with death in the name of eternal life is man's main task. The fundamental principle of ethics may be formulated as follows : act so as to conquer death and affirm everywhere, in everything and in relation to all, eternal and immortal life. It is base to forget the death of a single living being and to be reconciled to it. The death of the least and most miserable creature is unendurable, and if it is irremediable, the world cannot be accepted and justified. All and everything must be raised to eternal life. This means that the principle of eternal being must be affirmed in relation to human beings, animals, plants and even inanimate things. Man must always and in everything be a giver of life and radiate creative vital energy. Love for all that lives, for every creature, rising above the love for abstract ideas, means struggle against death in the name of eternal life. Christ's love for the world and for man is victory over the powers of death and the gift of abundant life.

Asceticism means struggle with death and with the mortal ele-

Death and Immortality

ments within oneself. Struggle with death in the name of eternal life demands such an attitude to oneself and to other people as though both I and they were on the point of death. Such is the moral significance of death in the world. Conquer the low animal fear of death, but always have a spiritual fear of it, a holy terror before its mystery. It was death that first gave man the idea of the supernatural. Enemies of religion such as Epicurus thought they disproved it by showing that it originated in the fear of death. But they will never succeed in disproving the truth that in the fear of death, in the holy terror of it, man comes into touch with the deepest mystery of being and that death contains a revelation. The moral paradox of life and of death can be expressed by a moral imperative : treat the living as though they were dying and the dead as though they were alive, i.e. always remember death as the mystery of life and always affirm eternal life both in life and in death.

Life, not in its weakness but in its strength, intensity and super-abundance, is closely connected with death. This is felt in the Dionysian cults. This is revealed in love which is always connected with death. Passion, i.e. the expression of the highest intensity of life, always holds the menace of death. He who accepts love in its overwhelming power and tragedy, accepts death. He who attaches too much value to life and avoids death, runs away from love and sacrifices it to other tasks of life. In erotic love the intensity of life reaches its highest pitch and leads to destruction and death. The lover is doomed to death and involves the loved one in his doom. In the second act of *Tristan and Isolde* Wagner gives a musical revelation of this. The herd-mind tries to weaken the connection between love and death, to safeguard love and settle it down in this world. But it is not even capable of noticing love. It organizes the life of the race and knows only one remedy against death—birth. Life seems to conquer death through birth. But the victory of birth over death has nothing to do with personality, with its fate and its hopes ; it is concerned with life of the race only. The victory over death through birth is an illusion. Nature does not know the mystery of conquering death ; the victory can come only from the supernatural world. Throughout their whole history men have tried to struggle against death, and this gave rise to various beliefs and theories. Sometimes the struggle took the form of forgetting about death and sometimes of idealizing it and revelling in the thought of destruction.

The philosophical idea of the natural immortality of the soul deduced from its substantiality leads nowhere. It ignores the fact of death and denies the tragedy of it. From the point of view of such a doctrine there is no need to struggle against death and corruption for the sake of eternal life. It is a rationalistic metaphysic without any tragic element in it. Scholastic spiritualism is not a solution of the problem of death and immortality, but is a purely abstract and academic theory. In the same way idealism does not solve the problem or indeed does not even face it. The idealism of the German metaphysics has no place for personality, regards it merely as a function of the world-spirit or idea, and therefore the tragedy of death does not exist for it. Death is a tragedy only when there is an acute awareness of personality. It is only because personality is experienced as eternal and immortal that death is felt to be a tragedy. The death of that which is eternal and immortal in its meaning and destination is alone tragic ; there is nothing tragic about the death of the temporal and the transitory. The death of personality in man is tragic because personality is God's eternal idea of him. It is unendurable that a complete personality containing the unity of all human powers and possibilities should die. Personality is not born of the father and the mother, it is created by God. There is no such thing as immortality of man as a natural being, born in the generic process ; there is no natural immortality of his soul and body. In this world man is a mortal being. But he is conscious of the Divine image and likeness in him and feels that he belongs not only to the natural but to the spiritual world as well. Man regards himself, therefore, as belonging to eternity, and yearns for eternity. What is eternal and immortal in man is not the psychical or the physical element as such but the spiritual element which, acting in the other two, constitutes personality and realizes the image and

324

likeness of God. Man is immortal and eternal as a spiritual being belonging to the incorruptible world, but his spirituality is not a naturally given fact ; man is a spiritual being in so far as he manifests himself as such, in so far as the spirit in him gains possession of the natural elements. Wholeness and unity result from the work of the spirit in the psychic and bodily elements and constitute personality. But the natural individual as such is not yet a personality, and immortality is not characteristic of him. Natural immortality belongs to the species or to the race but not to the individual. Immortality has to be won by the person and involves struggle for personality.

Idealism affirms the immortality of the impersonal or the superpersonal spirit, of the idea and value, but not of the person. Fichte and Hegel have nothing to say about personal human immortality. Human personality and its eternal destiny are sacrificed to the idea, the value, the world-spirit, world-reason, etc. There is an element of truth in this. It is true that it is not the natural, empirical man who is immortal and eternal but the spiritual, ideal, valuable element in him. The idealists, however, fail to recognize that this spiritual, ideal and valuable element forms an eternal personality and transmutes all man's powers for eternity ; they are wrong in separating it out and abstracting it into an ideal heaven as an impersonal and non-human spirit, abandoning the rest of man to death and corruption. A realized and completed personality is immortal. But in the spiritual world there are no self-contained personalities, they are united with God, with other personalities and with the cosmos.

Materialists, positivists and followers of similar theories accept death, legitimize it, and at the same time try to forget about it, building up life on the graves. Their views show a lack of " memory of death " and are therefore shallow and commonplace. The theory of progress is entirely taken up with the future of the species, of the race, of the coming generations, and has no concern with personality and its destiny. Progress, like evolution, is absolutely impersonal. For the progressing species death is an unpleasant fact, but one that has nothing deep or tragic about it. The species has an immortality of its own. It is only for the person and from the personal point of view that death is tragic and significant.

Theories of a nobler variety take up a sad and resigned attitude towards death. They recognize the tragic nature of it, but as conceived by them the human personality, though conscious of itself, has not the spiritual force to struggle with death and conquer it. The Stoic or the Buddhist attitude to death shows impotence in the face of it, but it is nobler than the naturalistic theories which completely ignore death. The emotional as distinct from the spiritual attitude to death is always melancholy and coloured by the sadness of memory which has no power to raise the dead ; only the spiritual attitude to death is victorious. The pre-Christian view of it implies resignation to fate. Christianity alone knows victory over death.

The ancient Hebrews were not familiar with the idea of personal immortality. We do not find it in the Bible. Personal self-consciousness had not yet awakened. The Jewish people were conscious of the immortality of their race but not of persons. Only in the book of Job there is awareness of personal destiny and its tragedy. It was not until the Hellenistic era, just before the coming of Christ, that the spiritual element in the Jewish religion came to be to some extent disentangled from the naturalistic, or, in other words, that personality was liberated and no longer dissolved in the collective, racial life. But the idea of immortality was truly revealed in the Greek and not in the Jewish thought.[1] The development of that idea in Greece is very instructive. At first man was recognized as mortal. Gods were immortal, but not men. Immortality was an attribute of the divine and not of the human nature. It came to be ascribed to man in so far as the divine, superhuman element was manifested in him. Not ordinary men but demigods, heroes and demons were immortal. The Greeks knew well the heartrending grief caused by death. Greek tragedy and poetry is full of it. Man was resigned to inevitable death ; he was denied

[1] See Erwin Rohde, *Psyche, Seelenkult und Unsterblichkeitsglaube der Griechen*.

326

immortality which the gods appropriated for themselves alone. The mortal human and the immortal divine principles were dissevered and became united only in heroes and supermen. Man descended into the subterranean realm of shadows and nothing could be sadder than his destiny. The melancholy, characteristic of the Greek and alien in this form to the Hebraic feeling for life, was rooted in the fact that the Greeks were able to reveal the human principle but not to connect it with the divine. It was the humanity of the Greeks that gave rise to the melancholy. And it was from the Greeks we heard the words that it was better for man not to be born. This is not the Indian metaphysical pessimism which denies man and regards the world as an illusion. It is an expression of human sadness for which both man and the world are real. Greeks were realists. But the Greek genius could not endure for ever the hiatus between the divine and the human world that doomed men to death and reserved immortality for the gods. A struggle for human immortality began.

The religious mythological consciousness of Greece recognized that although the divine principle was immortal and the human mortal, man's thought brought him into communion with the divine and enabled him to rise up to it and acquire it. This was the teaching of the Mysteries, of the Orphics and of Plato's philosophy. The human soul contains a divine element, but it must be freed from the power of matter ; only then will man become immortal. Immortality means that the divine element of the soul forsakes the lower, material world and does not transfigure it. Immortality is ideal and spiritual. It belongs only to that which is immortal in its metaphysical nature, but is not won for elements that are mortal and corruptible, i.e. death and corruption are not conquered. According to the Orphic myth the soul descends into the sinful material world, but it must be freed from it and return to its spiritual home. That myth had a great influence upon Plato, as can be seen particularly from *Phaedo*, and is one of the most profound human myths. It is connected with the ancient doctrine of reincarnation—one of the few attempts to understand the destiny of the soul in its past and future. And Orphism does contain a certain eternal truth. Christianity teaches of resurrection, of the victory over death for every life, for all the created world, and in this it is infinitely superior to the Greek conception of immortality which dooms a considerable part of the world to death and corruption. But the Christian view does not make clear the mystery of the genesis of the soul. The presence of the eternal element in the soul means eternity not only in the future but in the past as well. That which has an origin in time cannot inherit eternity. If the human soul bears the image and likeness of God, if it is God's idea, it arises in eternity and not in time, in the spiritual and not in the natural world. But Christian consciousness can interpret this dynamically and not statically as Platonism does. In eternity, in the spiritual world, there goes on a struggle for personality, for the realization of God's idea. Our natural earthly life is but a moment in the process which takes place in the spiritual world. This leads to the recognition of pre-existence in the spiritual world, which does not by any means involve reincarnation on earth.

The fact that man belongs to the eternal spiritual world does not imply a natural immortality of the spirit. Our natural world is the arena of the struggle for eternity and immortality, i.e. of the struggle for personality. In this struggle the spirit must gain possession of the natural elements of the soul and body for their eternal life and resurrection. Christianity teaches not so much of natural immortality which does not presuppose any struggle as of resurrection which presupposes the struggle of spiritual gracious forces with the powers of death. Resurrection means spiritual victory over death, it leaves nothing to death and corruption, as abstract spiritualism does. The doctrine of resurrection recognizes the tragic fact of death and means victory over it—which is not to be found in any doctrines of immortality, whether Orphic or Platonic or theosophical. Christianity alone faces death, recognizes both its tragedy and its meaning, but at the same time refuses to reconcile itself to it and conquers it. Eternal and immortal life is possible for man not because it is natural to the human soul, but because Christ rose from the dead and conquered the deadly powers of the world—because in the cosmic miracle of the Resurrection meaning has triumphed over meaninglessness.

The doctrine of the natural immortality of the human soul severs the destiny of the individual soul from the destiny of the cosmos, of the world-whole. It is metaphysical individualism. But the doctrine of the Resurrection links up the destiny of man with world-destiny. The resurrection of my body is at the same time the resurrection of the body of the world. " Body " in this connection means of course " spiritual body " and not the material frame. A complete personality is connected with the body and the eternal form of it and not merely with the soul. If it had not been for the coming of Christ and for His Resurrection, death would have triumphed in the world and in man. The doctrine of immortality is paradoxical : man is both mortal and immortal, he belongs both to the death-dealing time and to eternity, he is both a spiritual and a natural being. Death is a terrible tragedy, and death is conquered by death through Resurrection. It is conquered not by natural but by supernatural forces.

Two Russian religious thinkers have said remarkable things about life and death, from two entirely opposed points of view—V. Rozanov and N. Feodorov. For Rozanov all religions fall into two categories according as to whether they are based on the fact of birth or of death. Birth and death are the most important and significant events in life, and in the experience of them we catch a glimpse of the divine. Judaism and almost all pagan religions are for Rozanov religions of birth, while Christianity is the religion of death. Religions of birth are religions of life, since life springs from birth, i.e. from sex. But Christianity has not blessed birth, has not blessed sex, but enchanted the world with the beauty of death. Rozanov struggles against death in the name of life. In his view death is conquered by birth. Life is for ever triumphant through birth. But then death is conquered by life only for the newly born and not for the dead. To regard birth as victory over death is only possible if one is utterly insensitive to the human personality and its

329

eternal destiny. For Rozanov the primary reality and the bearer of life is the genus and not the individual. In birth the genus triumphs over the personality : the genus lives for ever, the person dies. But the tragic problem of death is the problem of personality and not of the genus, and it is experienced in all its poignancy when personality is conscious of itself as a true reality and the bearer of life. However flourishing the life of the new generations may be, it does not remedy the unendurable tragedy of the death of a single living being. Rozanov knows nothing about eternal life, he knows only the endless life through child-bearing. It is a kind of sexual pantheism. Rozanov forgets that it was not with Christ that death came into the world and that the last word of Christianity is not death, not Calvary, but Resurrection and eternal life. Rozanov seeks escape from the horror of death in the vital intensity of sex. But sex in its fallen state is the very source of death in the world, and it is not for it to conquer death.

For N. Feodorov the problem is quite different. No one in the whole of human history has felt such pain at the thought of death as did Feodorov, nor such a burning desire to restore to life all who died. While Rozanov thinks of the children that are being born and finds comfort in the thoughts of life in the future, Feodorov thinks of the dead ancestors, and finds a source of sorrow in the thought of death in the past. For Feodorov death is the worst and only evil. We must not passively resign ourselves to it ; it is the source of all evils. Final victory over death consists, in his view, not in the birth of a new life but in raising up the old, in bestowing resurrection upon the dead ancestors. This feeling for the dead shows how lofty was Feodorov's moral consciousness. Man ought to be a giver of life and affirm life for all eternity. This is the supreme moral truth, whatever we may think of Feodorov's " plan " of raising the dead.

There was a great deal of truth, but also a great deal of error, in Feodorov's attitude to death. He wrongly understood the mystery of it. Feodorov was a believing Christian, but he apparently failed to grasp the mystery of the Cross and to accept the redeeming meaning of death. Death was not for him an inner moment of life, through which every sinful life must inevitably pass. While Rozanov was blind to the Resurrection, Feodorov failed to see the Cross and its redeeming significance. Both wanted to struggle with death in the name of life and to conquer death—one through birth and the other through raising the dead to life. There is more truth in Feodorov's view, but it is a one-sided truth. Death cannot be conquered by denying all meaning to it, i.e. by denying its metaphysical depth. Heidegger rightly says that the source of death is " anxiety ", but that is a source visible from our everyday world. Death is also a manifestation of eternity, and in our sinful world eternity means terror and anguish. The paradoxical fact that a man may be afraid of dying in an accident or from a contagious disease, but is not afraid of dying on the battlefield or as a martyr for his faith, shows that eternity is less terrifying when we rise above the level of commonplace everyday existence.

Both individual death and the death of the world inspire horror. There is a personal and a cosmic Apocalypse. Apocalyptic mood is one in which the thought of death reaches its highest intensity, but death is experienced as the way to a new life. The Apocalypse is the revelation about the death of the cosmos, though death is not the last word of it. Not only the individual man is mortal, but also races, civilizations, mankind as a whole, all the world and all created things. It is remarkable that the anguish of this thought is even greater than that of the anticipation of personal death. The fate of the individual and of the world are closely interconnected and intertwined by thousands of bonds. Man suffers anguish not only because he is doomed to death but because all the world is doomed to it. During historical epochs which were not marked by apocalyptic moods a man's death was softened by the thought of the race continuing for ever and preserving the results of his life and activity. But Apocalypse is the end of all perspectives of racial or cosmic immortality ; in it every creature and all the world is directly faced with the judgment of eternity. There can be no comfort in the thought that we shall be immortal in our children and that our work will last for ever, for the end is coming to all consolations that are in time. Apocalypse is a paradox of time and eternity that cannot be expressed in rational terms. The end of our world will come in time, in time as we know it. But it is also the end of time as we know it and therefore lies beyond its limits. This is an antinomy similar to Kant's antinomies of pure reason.[1] When the end comes there shall be no more time. And therefore we must paradoxically think of the end of the world both as in time and in eternity. The end of the world, like the end of each individual man, is an event both immanent and transcendent. Horror and anguish are caused by this incomprehensible combination of the transcendent and the immanent, the temporal and the eternal. For every one of us and for the world as a whole there comes a catastrophe, a jump across the abyss, a mysterious escape from time which takes place in time. The death of an individual is also a deliverance from time taking place in time. If our sinful temporal world as we know it were endless, this would be an evil nightmare, just like the endless continuation of an individual life. It would be a triumph of the meaningless. And the presentiment of the coming end calls forth, together with horror and anguish, hope and expectancy of the final revelation and triumph of meaning. Judgment and valuation of all that has happened in the world is the final revelation of meaning. The Last Judgment of individuals and of the world, interpreted in an inner sense, is nothing other than the discovery of meaning and the affirmation of qualities and values.

The paradox of time and eternity exists for the destiny both of the world and of the individual. Eternal and immortal life may be objectified and naturalized, and then it is spoken of as life in the world beyond. It appears as a natural realm of being though different from ours. Man enters it after death. But eternal and immortal life regarded from within and not objectified is essentially different in quality from the natural and even the supernatural existence. It is a spiritual life, in which eternity is attained while

[1] Kant's genius is seen at its best in his treatment of the antinomies of pure reason. See *Kritik der reinen Vernunft, Die Antinomie der reinen Vernunft*.

still in time. If man's existence were wholly taken up into the spirit and transmuted into spiritual life so that the spiritual principle gained final possession of the natural elements of the body and the soul, death as a natural fact would not take place at all. The transition to eternity would be accomplished without the event which externally appears to us as death. Eternal life is revealed in time, it may unfold itself in every instant as an eternal present. Eternal life is not a future life but life in the present, life in the depths of an instant of time. In those depths time is torn asunder. It is therefore a mistake to expect eternity in the future, in an existence beyond the grave, and to look forward to death in time in order to enter into the divine eternal life. Strictly speaking, eternity will never come in the future—in the future there can only be a bad infinity. Only hell can be thought of in this way. Eternity and eternal life come not in the future but in a moment, i.e. they are a deliverance from time, and mean ceasing to project life into time. In Heidegger's terminology it means the cessation of " anxiety " which gives temporal form to existence.

Death exists externally as a certain natural fact which takes place in the future, and it signifies that existence assumes a temporal form, and life is projected into the future. Inwardly, from the point of view of eternity unfolded in the depths of the moment and not projected into time, death does not exist ; it is only an element in the eternal life. Death exists only " on this side of things ", in temporal being, in the order of nature. The unfolding of spirituality, the affirmation of the eternal in life and participation in a different order of being mean transcendence of death and victory over it. To transcend death and conquer it is not to forget it or be insensitive to it, but to accept it within one's spirit, so that it ceases to be a natural, temporal fact and becomes a manifestation of meaning which proceeds from eternity.

The personal and the cosmic Apocalypse bring to light our failure to fulfil eternal righteousness in life and are a triumph of righteousness in the dark world of sin. The death of the world and of individuals, of nations, civilizations, customs, historical forms of state and society, is a catastrophic reminder on the part of truth and righteousness of the fact that they have been distorted and not fulfilled. This is the meaning, too, of all great revolutions which indicate an Apocalypse within history, and the meaning of catastrophic events in the individual life. The Revelation about the coming of the antichrist and his kingdom shows that the Christian truth has not been fulfilled and that men are incapable and unwilling to realize it. Such is the law of spiritual life. If men do not freely realize the Kingdom of Christ, the kingdom of the antichrist will be brought about with necessity. Death comes to all life which does not fulfil the divine meaning and the divine truth. The triumph of irrationality is the revelation of meaning in the darkness of sin. Hence death, both cosmic and individual, is not merely a triumph of meaningless dark forces and a result of sin but also a triumph of meaning. It reminds man of the divine truth and does not allow unrighteousness to be eternal.

Theoretically, N. Feodorov was right in saying that the world and man could pass into eternal life without the catastrophe of the end and the Last Judgment, if humanity were fraternally united for the sake of the common task of realizing Christian righteousness and raising the dead.[1] But the world and mankind have gone too far in the path of evil, and judgment has come upon them already. Irrational, meonic freedom prevents the realization of Feodorov's " plan ". He was too optimistic and undervalued the forces of evil. But the affirmation of eternity, of eternal life for every being and for all creation, is a moral imperative. Act so that eternal life might be revealed to you and that the energy of eternal life should radiate from you to all creation.

Ethics must be eschatological. The question of death and immortality is fundamental to a personalistic ethics and confronts us in every act and every expression of life. Insensitiveness to death and forgetfulness of it, so characteristic of the nineteenth and twentieth century ethics, mean insensitiveness to personality and to its eternal destiny, as well as insensitiveness to the destiny of the world as a

[1] See *Filosofia obshtchago dela.*

whole. Strictly speaking, a system of ethics which does not make death its central problem has no value and is lacking in depth and earnestness. Although it deals with judgments and valuations, it forgets about the final judgment and valuation, i.e. about the Last Judgment. Ethics must be framed not with a prospect to happiness in an unending life here, but in view of an inevitable death and victory over death, of resurrection and eternal life. Creative ethics calls us not to the creation of temporary, transitory and corruptible goods and values which help us to forget death, the end, and the Last Judgment, but to the creation of eternal, permanent, immortal goods and values which further the victory of eternity and prepare man for the end.

Eschatological ethics does not by any means imply a passive renunciation of creative activity. Passive apocalyptic moods are a thing of the past, they are a sign of decadence and an escape from life. On the contrary, eschatological ethics based upon apocalyptic experience demands an unprecedented intensity of human creativeness and activity. We must not passively await in horror and anguish the impending end and the death of human personality and the world. Man is called actively to struggle with the deadly forces of evil and creatively to prepare for the coming of the Kingdom of God. Christ's second coming presupposes intense creative activity on our part, preparing both mankind and the world for the end. The end itself depends upon man's creative activity and is determined by the positive results of the cosmic process. We must not passively wait for the Kingdom of Christ, any more than for that of antichrist, but must actively and creatively struggle against the latter and prepare for the Kingdom of God which is taken by force.

To regard apocalyptic prophecies with passive resignation means to interpret them in a naturalistic sense, to rationalize them and deny the mysterious combination of Divine Providence and human freedom. It is equally wrong to take up a passive and fatalistic attitude to one's own death, to the death of personality, and regard it as a predetermined natural fact. We must accept death freely and with an enlightened mind, and not rebel against it ; but this free and enlightened acceptance of death is a creative activity of the spirit. There is a false activity which rebels against death and refuses to accept it. It leads to unendurable suffering. But there is also the true activity which is the victory of eternity over death. An active spirit does not really fear death—only a passive spirit does. An active spirit experiences an infinitely greater fear and terror than that of death—the fear of hell and eternal torments. It lives through its own eternity ; death exists for it not inwardly but merely as an external fact. It experiences terror at the thought of its eternal destiny and of the judgment which is in eternity.

We come here upon a psychological paradox which to many people is unknown and incomprehensible. An active spirit which has a direct inward experience of being eternal and indestructible may, so far from fearing death, actually desire it and envy those who do not believe in immortality and are convinced that death is the end. It is a mistake to imagine that the so-called faith in immortality is always comforting and that those who have it are in a privileged and enviable position. Faith in immortality is a comfort and makes life less hard, but it is also a source of terror and of an overwhelming responsibility. Those who are convinced that there is no immortality know nothing of this responsibility. It would be more correct to say that the unbelievers rather than the believers make life easy for themselves. Unbelief in immortality is suspicious just because it is so easy and comforting ; the unbelievers comfort themselves with the thought that in eternity there will be no judgment of meaning over their meaningless lives. The extreme, unendurable terror is not the terror of death but of judgment and of hell. It does not exist for the unbelievers, only the believers know it. A passive spirit seldom experiences it, but an active one experiences it with particular intensity, because it is apt to connect its destiny, and consequently judgment and the possibility of hell, with its own creative efforts. The problem of death inevitably leads to that of hell. Victory over death is not the last and final victory. Victory over death is too much concerned with time. The last, final and ultimate victory is victory over hell. It is wholly concerned with eternity.

Still more fundamental than the task of raising the dead, preached by Feodorov, is the task of conquering hell and freeing from it all who are suffering " eternal " torments. The final task, which ethics is bound to set us in the end, is creative liberation of all beings from the temporal and " eternal " torments of hell. If this task is not realized, the Kingdom of God cannot be realized either.

SCIENCE, RELIGION
AND SOCIALISM

Joseph Needham

Science, Religion and Socialism

(A contribution to the book of essays *Christianity and the Social Revolution*, 1935; with additions, including material from the Criterion, 1932, and Scrutiny, 1932.)

THE problem of the relationship between the traditional religion of the European West and the coming new world-order, as yet in its details uncertain, seems at first sight to have little to do with the preoccupations of the scientist. Whether the old forms of theology and liturgy disappear, whether the new social order is, or is not, more just than that which is breaking up, whether he has to live and work in the corporate or in the classless State, might seem to be matters of indifference to him. Nevertheless such a view would be superficial. The moment a scientific worker begins to reflect upon the nature and methods of his science, he will find himself involved in its history and philosophy, and hence its relations to historical, economic and intellectual factors, from which religious ideas certainly cannot be excluded. The moment he begins to reflect upon the ends to which others are putting the results of his work, he will find himself involved in the current political discussion of his time. Even some hypothetical scientist who aimed at the most complete neutrality with respect to the world in which he lived could not long escape the ultimate argument of economic forces, and would be induced to think over his relation to his fellows when he found himself unemployed after some sudden restriction of scientific effort.

The beginnings of the scientific movement in the 17th century are discussed elsewhere in this book. Acquisition of personal wealth, the fundamental motive of capitalist enterprise, acted then, and for a long time afterwards, as the most powerful stimulus and support for scientific research. But the indiscriminate application of the scientific method to natural things bursts in the end these limitations. It shows us not only how to make textiles and cheese, but also how, if we will, a high degree of universal physical and mental well-being may be achieved. In so doing, it goes beyond the facts which any single group of men can lay hold of with the object of acquiring private riches. And it dictates to the scientific worker a new allegiance, a separation from his allies (or masters) of three centuries standing.

The Position of the Scientific Worker.

The position of the scientific worker in the world of to-day is indeed a very difficult one. Owing to the gradual permeation of our entire civilisation by the practical results of scientific thought and invention, the scientific worker has in some measure succeeded to the semi-oracular tripod previously occupied by the religious thinker, whether enthusiastic saint or prudent ecclesiastic. That ancient separation of life into secular and sacred, which arose out of the acquiescence of the early christians in their failure to transform the human society of their time into God's Kingdom on earth, still reigns in our civilisation. Owing to the increasing intellectual difficulties which the ordinary man of our time feels with respect to the theology of the traditional form of western European religion, he turns more and more to the scientific worker, expecting to hear from *him* a sound doctrine about the beginning of the world, the duty of man, and the four last things. The scientific "ascetic" in the laboratory is the monk of to-day, and is tacitly regarded as such by the ordinary man.[1] Conversely, the secular power, the medieval *imperium*, has been succeeded by the power of the owner—the owner of factories, the owner of newspapers and propaganda agencies, the owner of land, the owner of finance capital.

In a new guise, then, the sacred and the secular are still at war. We may study their antagonism best by observing the fate of the concept of *Regnum Dei*, the Kingdom of God—always the surest indication of the relative power of priest and king. Roughly speaking, there have been, in the history of the Christian Church, three separate doctrines about the Kingdom of God, three separate interpretations of the Kingdom-passages in the Gospels.[2] First, there was the identification of the Kingdom with a purely spiritual mystical realm of beatitude, either to be reached after death by the faithful, or attainable here and now through the methods of prayer and ascetic technique, or existing in the future in Heaven after the last judgment. This has been perhaps the commonest theory. It has flourished whenever the secular was strong, since it discountenanced any attempt to improve the conditions of life on earth. As an instance, one could mention the mystical theology of lutheranism, whose founder held the world

---

[1] He may be called an "ascetic" in that he has often sacrificed for his intellectual calling those material benefits which Lord Birkenhead referred to as the "glittering prizes" of the capitalist system.

[2] Cf. Bishop A. Robertson, *Regnum Dei* (London, 1901). We shall discuss this subject in more detail below, p. 50.

to be utterly bad and irredeemable, a realm of Satan, from which the only escape was by means of religious exercises within the organised body of christians.[1] But, secondly, in every age there have been those who have interpreted the Kingdom as a state of divine justice in the future and in the world, to be attained by unceasing effort on the part of men and women. This struggle was the outcome of their thirst for social justice, and gave meaning to all martyrdoms since the beginning of the world.

In ages when ecclesiastical organisation was powerful, the visible Church itself, sharing the world with the temporal emperor in a condominium, could be identified with the Kingdom of God. This was a third interpretation. With the reformation and the splitting of the universal church into a thousand sects it lost its force.

But if the scientific worker is the modern representative of the mediaeval cleric, he finds himself in a relatively much worse position. Science in our time is not able to dictate its terms to capitalist "captains of industry" and the governing class in general; on the contrary, it is in utter bondage, dependent upon their fitful and grudging support, itself divided by dangerous national boundaries and sovereignties. In such a case we should expect that many scientists would interpret the concept of the Kingdom (though none of them, of course, would dream of referring to it under that name) as something spiritual, something harmless, something incapable of any affront to a capitalist world.

This is exactly what we find. Nothing could better illustrate the point than the Huxley Memorial Lecture of A. V. Hill, in 1933, and his subsequent controversy with J. B. S. Haldane—two of England's most distinguished biologists.[2] The discoveries of science, said Hill, whatever mistakes may be made, do gradually build up a structure which is approved by all sane men; in the last three hundred years, the experimental method, which is universal, has produced results beyond all previous human achievements. This universality of its method and results gives science a unique place among the interests of mankind. But "if scientific people are to be accorded the privileges of immunity and tolerance by civilised societies, they must observe

[1] See Pascal, R., The Social Basis of the German Reformation: Martin Luther and His Times (Watts, London, 1933).

[2] Hill, A. V., Huxley Memorial Lecture, 1933; abridged version: "International Status and Obligations of Science," Nature, 1933, 132, 952. Hill, A. V., and Haldane, J. B. S., Nature, 1934, 133, 65.

the rules." "Not meddling with morals or politics; such, I would urge," he went on, "is the normal condition of tolerance and immunity for scientific pursuits in a civilised state." Nothing would be worse than that science should become involved with emotion, propaganda, or particular social and economic theories. In other words—"My kingdom is not of this world," must be taken as meaning not *in* this world either. Let unemployment, repression, class justice, national and imperial wars, poverty in the midst of plenty, etc., etc., continue and increase; nothing is relevant to the scientific worker, provided only his immunity is granted—immunity to pursue his abstract investigations in peace and quiet. Here we substitute for the kingdom-concept of mysticism a kingdom-concept of mathematics, equally sterile with respect to human welfare, equally satisfactory to the powers of this world.

"The best intellects and characters, not the worst," continued Hill, "are wanted for the moral teachers and political governors of mankind, but science should remain aloof and detached, not from any sense of superiority, not from any indifference to the common welfare, but as a condition of complete intellectual honesty." Haldane was not slow to point out that Hill's sterilisation of the scientific worker as a social unit arose from the facile ascription to him of no loyalties save those of his work. In so far as he is a citizen as well as a scientist, he *must* meddle with morals and politics. But Hill's point of view can be attacked more severely from a deeper standpoint. Science does not exist in a vacuum; scientific discoveries are not made by an inexplicable succession of demiurges sent to us by Heaven; science is, *de facto*, involved with "particular social and economic theories," since it exists and has grown up in a particular social and economic structure. Here there is no space even to outline the marks which theoretical and applied science bears revealing its historical position. I merely wish to point out that it is not altogether surprising that the ordinary man expects some lead from the scientific worker in his capacity of citizen. In the Middle Ages, life was ruled by theology, hence the socio-political influence of the theologian; today it is ruled by science, hence the socio-political importance of the scientific worker.

The Treason of the Scholars.

Hill's conception of the Kingdom as a realm of truth and exact knowledge far removed from the affairs of human life has been most clearly formulated in our time by Julien Benda, in his book, *La Trahison des Clercs*.[1] The betrayal of our generation by the clerks, that is to say, by the scientists and scholars which it has produced, he conceives to consist in the fact that whereas the mediaeval clerk was wholly devoted to the working out of the implications of a transcendent truth, the modern clerk has no similar task, and therefore engages without hesitation in the political struggles of the time. "Our century," says Benda, "will be called the century of the intellectual organisation of political hatreds. That will be one of its great claims to fame in the history of human ethics." But does not Benda misread the attitude of the mediaeval clerk? Preoccupied by transcendent truths he might certainly be, but he was also very much concerned about economic relationships, and, by virtue of that fact alone, he *was* politically minded in the modern sense of the words. For modern politics bear no relation to the politics of the mediaeval world. A 13th-century theologian might well leave on one side the quarrels of petty princes about territorial jurisdiction or feudal honours, but he, on his own assumptions, could not, and did not, leave on one side the detailed economics of the commerce and finance of the time. Benda fails to realise that in our days there is no longer any distinction between politics and economics. What are the ferocious modern nationalisms which he describes with such force but devices engineered and operated by economic interests which do not wish co-operation and friendship between the common peoples of the world? What is jingo imperialist patriotism but an instrument designed to drown the call to union of the *Communist Manifesto?*

The mediaeval scene was supremely characterised by its subordination of other interests to religion. We may call it a period of religious genius, when all poetry, literature, learning, and music was co-opted into the service of this primary preoccupation of men. And since this was the case, no human interests could be regarded as outside the sphere of theology, least of all the interests of the market-place, where every economic transaction was a possible opportunity for the snares of the devil, or, alternatively, could, by right arrangement, be turned into an exercise of spiritual profit. The life of man on earth

---

[1] Benda, J., *La Trahison des Clercs* (Grasset, Paris, 1927). The word clerk meant originally any man who could read, an attainment chiefly confined in the Middle Ages to ecclesiastics major and minor, cf. the Book of Common Prayer: "the priest and clerks."

was regarded not as an end in itself, but as the preparation for a fuller life in Heaven, a fuller life which could not be entered into without the passport of justice, temperance, and piety. It was the province of theology, therefore, to regulate public economic affairs just as much as those of individual devotion. The most important means by which this was done were first, the principle of the just price, and, secondly, the prohibition of usury. Every commodity had its just price, based on the cost of its production, and allowing to its producer a margin of profit sufficient for him to live in that degree of comfort which was considered appropriate to his station. It was unchristian to force prices up in a time of scarcity, and thus to take advantage of the necessity of others; unchristian to allow prices to fall in time of glut, and so defraud honest merchants. Usury was prohibited alike by civil and canon law.[1] And the names of many other long obsolete misdemeanours, such as regrating, forestalling and engrossing, remain to show how the theologian systematised mediaeval economic transactions.[2]

What would happen to our present social structure, we might ask, if by some miracle the mediaeval Church were to have full power again, and all usury were prohibited, the principle of the just price exacted, and the restriction of profits renewed? We should, of course, observe a very spectacular collapse. The Middle Ages had, in fact, their own conception of collectivism, but it was fundamentally non-equalitarian. Each group, ecclesiastical, military, or commercial, held a distinct place in a system of social orders possessing different degrees of wealth and social prestige. And although it was true that each order had definite duties towards the other orders, not excluding even the peasant basis, it was equally true that these obligations were frequently unfulfilled. Still, mediaeval society was organic, rather than individualistic and atomic. As Chaucer's Parson said:

> "I wot well there is degree above degree, as reason is, and skill it is that men do their devoir thereas it is due, but certes extortions and despite of your underlings is damnable."

[1] Cf. W. Cunningham's *Christian Opinion on Usury* (Edinburgh, 1884).
[2] Regrating was the practice of buying goods in order to sell them again in the same market at a higher price, and without adding to their value. Forestalling was the purchase of goods on their way to the market, or immediately on their arrival, or before the market had properly opened, in order to get them more cheaply. Engrossing was the mediaeval counterpart of cornering, the buying up of the whole, or a large part, of the stock of a commodity in order to force up the price.

"The clerk can only be strong," says Benda, "if he is fully conscious of his nature and his function, and if he shows us that he is conscious of it, that is to say, if he declares to us that his kingdom is not of this world. This absence of practical value is precisely what gives greatness to his teaching. As for the prosperity of the kingdoms of this world, that belongs to the ethic of Caesar, and not to his ethic. And with this position the clerk is crucified, but he has won the respect of men and they are haunted by his words." Yet if one of Julien Benda's mediaeval clerks were placed in our modern world, would he not denounce the fantastic system of economics under which we live; would he not criticise the laws which cause food to be destroyed because people are too poor to buy it? It is well that Benda castigates the modern clerk for lending the weapons of his intellect to nationalism, but there are other forces than nationalism at work in the political world to-day. He can, of course, remain inactive, adopting the position of absolute neutrality laid down by Benda, and urged, as we have seen, by distinguished representatives of science, refusing to take part in the political and social struggle, and finally perishing, like an Archimedes, at his laboratory bench during a war. But what differentiates the position of the modern from the mediaeval clerk is that, if he was to be active, the latter had no choice in his allegiance, while the former has a choice, and must make it. Thus there are two ways open to the scientific worker at the present time. All the backward pull of respectability and tradition urges him to throw in his lot with the existing capitalist order, with its corollaries of nationalism, imperialism, militarism, and, ultimately, fascism. On the other hand, he can adopt the ideals of social justice and of the classless State; he can recognise that his own best interests lie with the triumph of the working-class, the only class pledged to abolish classes; in a word, he can think of the Kingdom *literally* and can work for its realisation. A Kingdom not of this world, but to be in this world.

The transcendent truth of the mediaeval Church was bound up with a definite economic order, feudalism; and it was capitalism, of course, as it gradually developed, which upset this economic order, and science which superseded this transcendent truth. The geographical discoveries, which made the European home begin to seem a prison; the astronomical discoveries, which made the earth as a whole, previously the scene of the drama of redemption, shrink to one among a vast number of celestial bodies; the mechanical discoveries which opened up the possibility of industrialism; all undermined the strength of the old-fashioned system until hardly anything was left of it. Moreover, there were discoveries in the spiritual world, too; there was the important protestant discovery that material riches, far from being a presumptive sign of ill dealings, were an outward and visible sign of the inward approval and blessing of God. And most interesting of all, there was the rise of the concept of scientific law, often conceived of in a crude mechanical way, as was only natural at its first beginnings. Who would connect with this the decline in the cult of the Blessed Virgin? Yet there was a certain connection. "The Virgin," wrote Henry Adams,[1] "embarrassed the Trinity. Perhaps this was the reason why men loved and adored her with a passion such as no other deity has ever inspired. Mary concentrated in herself the whole rebellion of man against fate; the whole protest against divine law; the whole contempt of man for human law as its outcome; the whole unutterable fury of human nature beating itself against the walls of its prison-house, and suddenly seized by a hope that in the Virgin there was a door of escape. She was above law; she took a feminine pleasure in turning hell into an ornament, as witness the west window at Chartres; she delighted in trampling on every social distinction in this world and in the next. She knew that the universe was as unintelligible to her, on any theory of morals, as it was to her worshippers, and she felt, like them, no sure conviction that it was any more intelligible to the creator of it. To her, every suppliant was a universe in himself, to be judged apart, on his own merits, by his love for her—by no means on his orthodoxy or his conventional standing in the Church, or his correctness in defining the nature of the Trinity." What a collapse it was when men came to feel that this way of escape was no longer open to them. As canon law decayed, as confidence in the absoluteness and divine authority of civil law disappeared, so scientific law arose like the growing light of day. The mediaeval worship of Mary, so charming, so naïve, was a phenomenon of childhood. She could perhaps save a suppliant from a ruling, a decretal, or a codex, but not from the laws of gravitation or thermodynamics. Mankind was now to take up again the guidance of old Epicurus—

> "Hunc igitur terrorem animi tenebrásque necessest
> non radii solis, neque lucida tela diei ,
> discutiant, sed naturae species ratioque."[2]

[1] Henry Adams, *Mont St. Michel and Chartres*, Massachusetts Historical Society, p. 276. [2] *De Rer. Nat.* VI, 39

(These terrors then, this darkness of the mind,
Not sunrise with its flaring spokes of light,
Nor glittering arrows of morning can disperse,
But only Nature's aspect and her law.)

The path lay open now towards a surer freedom, if first necessity could be understood. Amid such vast changes of intellectual climate, it is not surprising that the function of the clerk should both change and yet remain the same.

The Concept of the Kingdom.

The concept of the Kingdom is of such importance for every aspect of the relations between christianity and communism that I must amplify a little what I said above about the forms which it has taken in christian thought. We may divide the logical possibilities into four. The Kingdom of God has been thought to exist:

(1) Here and now;
(2) Here but not yet;
(3) Not here but now already;
(4) Not here and not yet.

Clearly the most fundamental distinction lies between those who have looked for the Kingdom on earth, whether now or in the future, and those who have interpreted it as meaning an essentially invisible and other-worldly state. The extremest division lies between the second and third alternatives.

The early Church, which for this purpose must be taken as meaning up to the end of the 3rd century in the east and the end of the 4th in the west, was almost wholly devoted to the second of these interpretations. It was believed that the second coming of the Lord, which was thought to be imminent, would inaugurate a visible reign of complete righteousness, in which the saints would administer, until the last judgment, a society based on love and justice. This doctrine, known to theologians as millenniarism, chiliasm, or "realistic eschatology," found its canonical authority largely in the Apocalypse of John, and its intellectual defenders in such men as Cyprian, Justin, Irenaeus and Tertullian. It was attacked, as time went on, by three principal factors. First, there was the necessity of adapting the prophetic vision of a world made new to a world in which the expected leader did not return. Secondly, there was the influence of Hellenistic mysticism and allegorisation, which in the hands of Origen and other more thorough-going neo-platonists, tended to emphasise the third interpretation, i.e. that the Kingdom was a purely mystical idea, existing now but elsewhere, wholly in the world of the spirit. Thirdly, there was the increasing organisation of the Church, and the acceptance of this by the secular power in the time of Constantine; this invited men to diminish their ideals of love and justice, and to identify the Kingdom with an actually existing society. This led to the first interpretation. The Kingdom was "here and now," either in the form of the Eastern Empire or the Latin Church, which after Augustine claimed, and still claims officially to this day, to be itself the Kingdom. Lastly in all the ages of christianity there have been supporters of the fourth and most utterly remote interpretation, namely that the Kingdom means only the reign of God after the last judgment.

The millenniarist viewpoint was essentially a continuation of the great strain of Hebrew prophecy, with which all the actors in the drama of the Gospels, whether known or unknown to us, had certainly been familiar. In this the reality of the time process was quite central. Take, for example, the following passage from Amos:[1]

"Hear this, O ye that would swallow up the needy and cause the poor of the land to fail, saying, When will the New Moon be gone that we can sell corn? and the Sabbath, that we may set forth wheat? making the measure small and the payment great, and dealing falsely with balances of deceit; that we may buy the poor for silver and the needy for a pair of shoes. . . . The Lord hath sworn by the excellency of Jacob, Surely I will never forget any of their works. . . . I will slay the last of them with the sword; there shall not one of them flee away. Though they dig into hell, thence shall mine hand take them; and though they climb up into heaven, thence will I bring them down. . . . But in that day I will raise up the tabernacle of David that is fallen, and close up the breaches thereof; and I will raise up his ruins and build it as in the days of old. Behold, the days come, saith the Lord, that the ploughman shall overtake the reaper, and the treader of grapes him that soweth seed; and the mountains shall drop sweet wine, and all the hills shall melt." It is extremely interesting to contrast the Hebrew apocalyptic conviction that in the future evil will be overthrown and the earth become a common and bountiful treasury for a right-loving people, with the characteristically Hellenic belief in a former Golden Age from which humanity has for ever

[1] Chapter viii. 9.

fallen away. The only other ancient literature which has resemblances to that of the Hebrews in this respect is the Chinese, where remarkable descriptions of social evolution occur in the *I-Ching*, the "Book of Changes" (4th or 5th century B.C.). Hesiod, on the other hand, says that if it had not been for the act of Prometheus, who stormed heaven by force, brought thence the gift of fire, and provoked the gods to withhold from men an easy way of life, "you would have been able to do easily in a day enough work to keep you for a year, to hang up your rudder in the chimney corner, and let your fields run to waste."

Thus have decayed the first bright hopes and visions of the christians. In a most interesting passage, Bishop Robertson reveals the class character of the opposition to millenniarism. "Intense as was the christian instinct to which millenniarism gave articulate form, it was in some respects in latent antipathy to the ecclesiastical spirit, and waned as that spirit gathered strength. Its rejection by rational theology, and by the trained theologians who filled the more important places in the Greek Churches in the third and fourth centuries, had practically the effect of ranging the clergy in opposition to it. In fact, millenniarism, by virtue of its direct appeal to minds of crass simplicity, was a creed for the lay-folk and the simpler sort. When religious interest was concentrated upon it, it would indirectly undermine the interest felt in doctrines requiring a skilled class to interpret them. The apocalyptic spirit is in fact closely akin to the spirit of unregulated prophesying, and the alliance has been apparent, not only in the second century, but in mediaeval and modern times as well." Crass simplicity—might we not almost say inferior economic position? A skilled class—perhaps a privileged one too?

Of the hopes of the "simpler sort" we get a glimpse in that very interesting fragment of Papias, preserved by Irenaeus[1] and believed to be an authentic saying of Christ himself.[2] "The days will come when vines shall grow, each having ten thousand branches, and on each branch ten thousand twigs, and on each twig ten thousand shoots, and on each one of the shoots ten thousand clusters, and on every cluster ten thousand grapes, and every grape when pressed will give twenty-five firkins of wine. And when any one of the saints shall lay hold upon a cluster, another shall cry out, 'I am a better cluster; take me; bless the Lord through me.' And in like manner, that a

[1] See the *Apocryphal New Testament*, ed. M. R. James (Oxford, 1924, p. 36).
[2] "Old men who knew John the Lord's disciple, remember that they heard from him how the Lord taught concerning those times, saying, etc."

grain of wheat will produce ten thousand stalks, and each stalk ten thousand ears, . . ." and so forth.[1] It has often been said that the communism of the early christians was purely one of distribution, not of production. Here, however, we have, as it were, a dream of the abundance of natural wealth latent in the world's productive forces, and to be unloosed by science so many centuries later.[2] But the inevitable answering note is struck. Asceticism comes to the aid of the possessing classes, and when we turn to Augustine we find: "The opinion that the saints are to rise again would at least be tolerable if it were understood that they would enjoy spiritual delights from the presence of the Lord. We ourselves were formerly of this opinion. But when they say that those who then arise will spend their time in immoderate carnal feastings—in which the quantity of food and drink exceeds the bounds not only of all moderation, but of all credibility—such things cannot possibly be believed except by carnal persons."

Whatever happened in later centuries, then, it is certain that the christians of the primitive church put their Kingdom on the earth and in the future. To this belief of "crass simplicity" let us return. We reach the paradox that Marx and Engels would have been more acceptable to the martyrs and the Fathers than the comfortable 19th century theologians contemporary with them, seeking to excuse and support the phenomena of class oppression. For the kingdom of Marx was not of this world, but to be in this world.

Yet Benda goes on: "I regard as being able to say 'my kingdom is not of this world' all those whose activities do not pursue practical ends, the artist, the metaphysician, the scientist in so far as he finds satisfaction in the exercise of his science and not in its results. Many will tell me that these are the true clerks, much more than the christian, who only embraces the ideas of justice and love in order to win salvation." Here he adopts, as I think, a quite unjustifiable separation of these activities from practical affairs. In science, at any rate, the closest relations exist between practical technology and pure research.

---

[1] Similar accounts occur in the Jewish *Apocalypse of Baruch* and the Coptic *Apocalypse of James*.

[2] "So when the Lord was telling the disciples about the future kingdom of the saints, how glorious and wonderful it would be, Judas was struck by his words and said, 'Who shall see these things?' And the Lord said: 'These things shall they see who are worthy.' " (Hippolytus, *On Daniel*, 4.) "Papias says that when Judas the traitor believed not and asked, 'How then shall these growths be accomplished by the Lord?', the Lord said: 'They shall see who shall come thereto.' " (Irenaeus, *Contra Haer*, 5.)

Biology would be in an etiolated condition if it were not bound up at every point with stockbreeding, agriculture, medicine, the fisheries, and sociology. With physics and chemistry the case is even more obvious. "Historically, the sciences grow out of practice, the production of ideas arises out of the production of things."[1] It is true that in science we must not set out, in general, to solve problems *because* the answer will afford some new invention, but it is often the technical practice which suggests the problem. The great difference which we must recognise between mediaeval theology and modern science, is that an economic structure was directly and logically derivable from the former, and no clear system in such matters has as yet arisen from the latter. The former incorporated a system of ethics, in the form of moral theology. The latter has not as yet produced one.

Where, then, is the moral theology of to-day? The only possible answer is that communism provides the moral theology appropriate for our time.[2] The fact that a doctrine of God is apparently absent from it is unimportant in this connection; what it does is to lay down the ideal rules for the relations between man and man, to affirm that the exploitation of one class by another is immoral, that national wars for markets are immoral, that the oppression of subject and colonial races is immoral, that the unequal distribution of goods, education, and leisure is immoral, that the private ownership of the means of production is immoral. It dares to take the "love of our neighbour" literally; to ensure that by the abolition of privilege each single citizen shall have the fullest opportunities to live the good life in a community of free and equal colleagues. It continues and extends the historic work of christianity for woman, setting her on a complete equality with man. Its concept of leadership is leadership from within, not from above.

Only because christian theology three centuries ago gave up the attempt to apply a very similar ethic to human affairs has this state of things come about. The essential weakness of the modern clerk resides in the fact that vast progress in art or science appears at first sight to be theoretically equally compatible with national capitalism or with international communism. The economic doctrines which he

[1] Bukharin, N., *Theory and Practice from the Standpoint of Dialectical Materialism* (Kniga, London, 1931, p. 5).
[2] Cf. for example the essay "Communism and Morality" by A. L. Morton in *Christianity and the Social Revolution*, 1935, and "Marxism and Morality" by J. Hunter in University Forward, 1941, 6, 4.

must adopt are not at first sight a direct consequence of his own fundamental axioms, but embody themselves in a social theory external to his own sphere. Hence the dual character of the scientific worker, as scientist and as citizen. Hence the temptation for him to shirk his public responsibilities and as "pure clerk" to be silent except when he gives the results of his own exact researches.

We may remember the bitter words said to have been prefixed by the mathematician, G. H. Hardy, to a book on pure mathematics: "This subject has no practical value, that is to say, it cannot be used to accentuate the present inequalities in the distribution of wealth or to promote directly the destruction of human life."

Perhaps the most important task before scientific thinkers to-day is to show in detail how the ethics of collectivism do in fact emerge from what we know of the world and the evolutionary process that has taken place in it. Scientific socialism (I believe) is the only form of socialism which has the future before it; its theoreticians must therefore show not only that high levels of human social organisation have arisen and will arise by a continuation of the natural process, but what are the ethics appropriate to them. Scientific ethics should be to communist society what catholic ethics were to feudal society and protestant ethics to capitalist society.

Theology and the Modern Man.

In the preceding section I said that a doctrine of God was apparently absent from communist thought. I used the word "apparently" because (a) dialectical materialism might be logically compatible with a spinozistic theology;[1] (b) the immanence of the christian Godhead as Love is better provided for in communism than in any other order of human relationships. Future communist Clements of Alexandria will have the task of codifying the *praeparatio evangelica* of the christian centuries.

Today we are all Taoists and Epicureans. For the taoists, the Way of Nature was *tzu-jan* (自 然); it came *of itself*. So also in Lucretius' great poem[2]:

> ". . . natura videtur
> libera continuo dominis privata superbis
> ipsa sua per se sponte omnia dis agere expers."

---

[1] Cf. *Moscow Dialogues* by J. Hecker (London, 1933), p. 55, and *Fundamental Problems of Marxism*, by G. Plekhanov (ed. D. Riazanov, London, 1928), pp. 9 ff.
[2] *De Rer. Nat.* II, 1090.

(Nature, delivered from every haughty Lord
And forthwith free, is seen to do all things
Herself, and through herself of her own accord,
Free of all Gods.)

On the one hand there is the cosmic force which is "responsible" for the vast evolutionary process wherein we form a part, if anything is responsible for it. The modern mind finds the ancient scholastic arguments for the existence of this force or "prime mover" in no way convincing, still less that it partakes of the nature of what we call "mind" or "personality," and even less still that its essence is good. The good seems to arise out of the evolutionary process rather than to have been in it from the beginning. But the good is an immediate datum, and the holiness of good actions is an immediate datum. These are the occasions of modern religion.

From this point of view, the bonds of love and comradeship in human society are analogous to the various forces which hold particles together at the colloidal, crystalline, molecular, and even sub-atomic levels of organisation. The evolutionary process itself supplies us with a criterion of the good. The good is that which contributes most to the social solidarity of organisms having the high degree of organisation which human beings do in fact have. The original sin which prevents us from living as Confucius and Jesus enjoined[1] is recognisable as the remnants in us of features suitable to lower levels of social organisation; anti-social now. If such an idea is accepted, the insistence that we must have some extra-natural criterion of ethical values ceases to have any point. The kind of behaviour which has furthered man's social evolution in the past can be seen very well by viewing human history; and the great ethical teachers, from Confucius onwards, have shown us, in general terms, how men may live together in harmony, employing their several talents to the general good. Perfect social order, the reign of justice and love, the *Regnum Dei* of the theologians, the "Magnetic Mountain" of the poets, is a long way in the future yet, but we know by now the main ethical principles which will help us to get there, and we can dimly see how these have originated during social and biological evolution. There is no need for perplexity as to whether we ought to call evolution morally

---

[1] There is, of course, the incidental difficulty of continually modifying the letter of the teaching of the great ethical "mutants" to fit changing techniques and increasing knowledge, without losing their spirit.

admirable or morally offensive; it is surely neither. The good is a category which does not emerge until the human level is reached.[1]

The difficulty about religion is that it cannot be considered apart from organised religion as embodied in institutions.[2] In practice, its effects throughout the world are, in the present social context, largely harmful. How far religion can be transformed without the disappearance of the old vessels is a very disputable matter. The detailed beliefs of the past—verbal inspiration, eternal damnation, magical efficacy of prayer for "particular mercies" (in the old phrase), *ex opere operato* rites, miraculous intervention, ascription of psychological states to God, and so on, *are* of course irrevocably of the past, not of the present or the future. None of them are relevant to true religion. Religion is seen not as a divine revelation, but as a function of human nature, in Julian Huxley's words, as a "peculiar and complicated function, sometimes noble, sometimes hateful, sometimes intensely valuable, sometimes a bar to individual or social progress, but no more and no less a function of human nature than fighting or falling in love, than law or literature."[3] Theology, indeed, comes off badly in our modern survey. In so far as it is a codification of the experiences of religious mysticism it is an attempt to reduce to order what cannot be so reduced. In so far as it is a description of such experiences, it is engaged on the fruitless task of describing the indescribable. And in so far as it is occupied with cosmology, anthropology, and history, it is trespassing on legitimate fields of scientific activity.

Many students of these problems at the present time see that the essence of religion is the sense of the holy (Julian Huxley,[4] J. M. Murry,[5] Canon J. M. Wilson and others). Religion thus becomes no more and no less than the reaction of the human spirit to the facts of human destiny and the forces by which it is influenced; and natural piety, or a divination of sacredness in heroic goodness, becomes the primary religious activity. Consider also the following words of one of our most judicious philosophers:—"The identification of this-worldly with material values, other-worldly values alone being recognised as spiritual, is what I am concerned to deny. I maintain that

[1] In this connection C. M. Williams' *Review of the Systems of Ethics founded on the Theory of Evolution* (London, 1893), is still not without value.

[2] Cf. Lenin's remarks on religion in *Works*, Vol. 11, pp. 658 ff. and *Lenin on Religion* (Lawrence, London, n.d.).

[3] J. S. Huxley *What Dare I Think?* (Chatto and Windus, London, 1931), p. 187.

[4] loc. cit.

[5] J. M. Murry, many articles in the Adelphi, and especially 1932, 3, 267.

spiritual good and evil are to be found in the daily intercourse of men with one another in this world, independently of any relation of man to God; further, that the significance of spiritual value does not depend on God or upon the continuance of human beings after the death of the body."[1]

These opinions are not indeed very different from those of many modernist and liberal theologians. The difficulty about religion within the framework of organised christianity is that the "plain statements in Bible and Prayer-Book stand uncorrected and un-annotated," so that for simple people they mean what they say. For liberal intellectuals, this may be myth, that may be symbol, this may be a valiant attempt to express the inexpressible, that may be an unfortunate inexactitude due to historical causes—but for the majority of people, everything must be taken literally or not at all. Critics, then, have no alternative but to stand outside the traditional Church and give it advice from a distance, so that their remarks acquire a remote and impractical character. But an acquaintance with the life of religion from the inside convinces one that the sense of the holy cannot be ordered about at will, unhooked from one thing and hooked on to something else, or simply detached from ancient traditions and poured into the cold vacuum of our modern mechanical world. The poetic words of the Liturgy, for instance, philosophically meaningless though they may be, cannot be separated from the numinous feeling which has grown up with them. Though built upon the basis of a world-view which we can no longer accept to-day, they retain, for some of us, enough symbolism of what we *do* believe, to make them of overwhelming poetic value[2].

The upshot of the matter is, therefore, that in practice those who can successfully combine traditional religious life with the life of social and political action appropriate to our time, will be relatively few. It is no good being in a hurry to descry and to welcome the new forms of social emotion; they will emerge in their own good time and perhaps we shall not live to see them. But meanwhile, like the last Pontifex Maximus in Rome,[3] we shall continue those ancient rites which still have meaning for us, while nevertheless being on the best of terms with the clergy and people of the New Dispensation.

[1] Susan Stebbing, *Ideals and Illusions* (London, 1940), p. 31.

[2] Cf. Stewart D. Headlam's *The Service of Humanity* (London, 1882) and *The Meaning of the Mass* (London, 1905).

[3] Or the last priest of Zeus in Richard Garnett's story, *The Twilight of the Gods*. First published 1888, now in Thinker's Library Edition No. 81 (Watts, London, 1940).

Few would wish to maintain to-day that the organised religion of christianity has any gift of temporal immortality, and that it will not find its end just as the religions of ancient Egypt, or of Mexico, found theirs. But some would certainly wish to maintain that religion, as a natural department of the human spirit, has survived these changes and will always survive them. It could also be held that no historic religious system has failed to contribute some element of advance to man's social consciousness. The hope of making religion philo-sophically respectable is probably quite vain, and the sense of the holy in its ancient form cannot flourish in pure isolation away from its ancient trellis. But will not christian feeling be succeeded by another form of numinous feeling; a new development of social emotions? Even to ask this question is to ask where it could come from. We may be certain that it will not come from the lecture-rooms of academic philosophy, still less from the armchairs of literary critics or the speculations of scientific workers interested in religion from the outside. Will it not come from the factory? Obviously not the factory as we know it to-day, but the factory of the future, the factory of co-operating producers, when the whole system of com-mercial exploitation has been completely destroyed, and the means of production have been taken over in communal ownership. The most appalling struggles may well be involved in the death-throes of the present system, and we may perhaps expect that the numinous feeling of the future will take its origin from the consequent stress and strain. Is not Mayakovsky's poetry, are not the "Twelve" of Alexander Blok, the symbols of this? But meanwhile, Religion is still resident in her traditional house, and those who would seek her successfully must seek her there as well as in the leaflet distribution and the Trade Union Hall. Auden's words express what is going on:—

> "Love, loath to enter
> The suffering winter,
> Still willing to rejoice
> With the unbroken voice
> At the precocious charm
> Blithe in the dream
> Afraid to wake, afraid
> To doubt one term
> Of summer's perfect fraud,
> Enter and suffer
> Within the quarrel

59

Be most at home,
Among the sterile, prove
Your vigours, love.

Those of us who have loved the habitation of God's house and the place where his honour dwells, would be well content if the traditional forms of rite and liturgy could survive the coming storm.[1] We would like to fill the old bottles of Catholic doctrine with new wine. The words of the Fathers on equality and social righteousness seem more likely to be fulfilled than we had hoped. But if this revivification of the ancient faith cannot be accomplished, then we shall accept the judgment with a *Nunc dimittis*; those who love both the spirit and the letter will not complain if the spirit be taken and the letter left.

Before leaving the question of the possible forms which numinous feeling may take in future ages, a word should be said of the part which dramatic representations are likely to play. Cinema films of great power (such as Eisenstein's celebrated "Cruiser Potemkin") and also many documentary films portraying the natural and normal life of mankind in its struggle against the external world and its attainment of inner solidarity (such as the "Night Mail" of Grierson and Auden), generate in those who see them emotions to which it would be dangerous to refuse the term "numinous." After all, the religious origins of drama are well known, and it is surely significant that in the Soviet Union, the first great socialist state the world has ever seen, drama, poetry, and all cognate arts flourish as never before.[2] The catharsis of tragedy is only an extreme form of the effect upon individual human beings which any dramatic representation based on fundamental common human values must necessarily have. As the following interesting passage shows, religious exhortations in the old sense will not be needed in the future to awaken men to a sense of their social duty:

"In one of the novels of Ilya Ehrenburg there is a description of a play given by a travelling company at a collective farm somewhere in northern Russia. Othello was to be played, and the actress who was to take the part of Desdemona (the only

[1] Cf. what George Tyrrell said: "Houtin and Loisy are right; the christianity of the future will consist of mysticism and love, and possibly the Eucharist in its primitive form as the outward bond" (*Autobiography and Life*, London, 1912, vol. 2, p. 377).

[2] Cf. the article on the theatre in the Soviet Union by Herbert Marshall (University Forward, 1941, 7, 10).

sophisticated person present) felt that it was rather absurd. The collective farm had its usual anxieties; the cows were giving only half the amount of milk expected, the ploughing was backward, the fields of mangold-wurzels (or whatever it was) were covered with weeds and badly hoed. In the company's repertory there were Soviet plays, but the provincial actor-manager wanted to strut and gesticulate in the role of the jealous Moor, and nothing else would do. The play began by being misunderstood, but ended with great general emotion in the midst of tears and enthusiastic applause. The peasants of the collective farm were especially affected by Desdemona, but after the performance they amazed her, and even made her cry, because, instead of congratulating her on her acting, they made all kinds of unexpected promises about the augmentation of the milk yield, the improved cultivation of the fields, and the attainment of more than their scheduled production."[1]

Thus even farm labourers, at a comparatively low level of education and culture, could pass over very well from the emotion generated by the tragic situation of individuals, to that involved in the common situation of humanity. Not a few marxist thinkers have, as a matter of fact, foreseen the replacement of organised religion by the arts and drama.[2] This is possible not because the numinous is identical with the aesthetic, but because the never-ending tale of human relationships in the successive stages of social evolution and progress, can itself be the bearer of the numinous. As Feuerbach would have said, man will in this way realise that in the ideological structures of the traditional religions, he was really looking at himself and his own fate and the fate of his society.

Enemies of Human Experience.

There is a kind of fundamental validity attaching to the five great realms of human experience, philosophy, history, science, art, and religion. Each of these has its enemies—those who go about to deny their validity, or their right to exist, or their right to play the part which they do play in our civilisation or our individual lives. Let us consider some of these factors in relation to our main theme.

Against Philosophy come many opponents. Particularly, the

---

[1] From an essay by a Polish writer, Andrzej Stawar, which a Polish friend of mine and I translated together (Scrutiny, 1937, 6, 21).

[2] Especially G. Plekhanov, *Fundamental Problems of Marxism* (London, n.d.), p. 143.

mathematical logicians point out to us, that there are few, perhaps no, metaphysical propositions which can be translated into the exact language of mathematical logic. Philosophy on this view is an art, a sort of music gone wrong. Among these opponents, however, marxist ethics and orthodox theology cannot be numbered. They, at least, cannot be accused of undervaluing philosophy.

Against Science come many influences, some of which are equally opposed to philosophy. The whole anti-intellectualist movement, so protean in its manifestations in our time, acts in this direction. From the mystical point of view represented by D. H. Lawrence and his followers at one end to the folky-brutal atmosphere of nazism at the other, we have a thoroughly anti-scientific front. For these minds, if so they can be called, scientific internationalism is an illusion, racial factors dominate human actions, and true patriots must think with their blood. Nothing could be more valuable for the armament manufacturers than these views; nothing could be more in line with the feudal vestiges which have for centuries lingered on in the army-officer class. We are witnessing at the present day a wholesale frustration of science.[1] To the capitalist, scientific research is useful, but only relatively in comparison with other and perhaps even cheaper ways of obtaining profits. It is only when these fail that the capitalist now needs the scientist. Again, the conditions of profit-making forbid the introduction of safety measures and the application of labour-saving devices which could greatly increase world-production, while at the same time equalising leisure in the form of a five-hour day under a planned socialist system. Or improved technical methods may be used for actually destroying a part of the produced material, such as coffee or rubber. Or the area of land sown may be compulsorily restricted. Worst of all, perhaps, is the continuing and increasing use of science in war preparations; the development and application of the most diverse scientific researches to rendering the· killing of individuals more effective, cheaper, and possible on a still larger scale than ever before. "It does not need much economic knowledge," writes Bernal,[2] "to see that a system of which the essential basis is production for profit, leads by its own impetus into the present highly unstable and dangerous economic and political situation, where

---

[1] See the book of essays, *The Frustration of Science*, by Sir Daniel Hall, J. D. Bernal, J. G. Crowther, E. Charles, V. H. Mottram, P. Gorer, and B. Woolf (Allen & Unwin, London, 1934).

[2] Bernal, J. D., "National Scientific Research," *Progress*, 1934, **2**, 364.

SCIENCE RELIGION AND SOCIALISM

plenty and poverty, the desire for peace and the preparation for war, exist side by side; but it does require far more knowledge to see how an alternative system could be built up. And yet, unless scientists are prepared to study this they must accept the present state of affairs and see the results of their own work inadequately utilised to-day and dangerously abused in the near future." Thus the figures of the annual government grants speak for themselves. In 1933, for example, the Medical Research Council received £139,000 and the Department for Scientific and Industrial Research £443,838, while the research grants for the Army, Navy, and Air Force together were £2,759,000, i.e. five times as much as the whole total for civil research.[1]

Another of the influences working in our time against science is the outcome of modern psychology.[2] An argument nowadays need not be answered; it is sufficient to trace it back to the previous psychological history, and hence the prejudices, of the person who propounds it. A misunderstanding of marxism, with its insistence upon the class basis of science, has exposed it to this accusation, but it is perfectly legitimate to apply the class theory of history to the history of science, and the results are frequently highly convincing. On the other hand the fascist struggle (especially in Germany) against "objective science," based on the racial theory of history, which has no scientific basis of any sort, is the most dangerous form of this kind of attack which exists, though it can only be seriously proclaimed to the masses under conditions where all criticism is silenced by state power. As for Art, it does not pay.[3] No further enemy is needed. And History, as eminent capitalists have assured us, is bunk.[4]

Against Religion come so many forces that it is hard to count them. The general trend from religion to science which took place in the Hellenistic age and the late Roman Empire repeated itself again in our own western European civilisation from the Renaissance onwards. Religion has had to face the great pretensions of the mediaeval secular power, the mechanical philosophies of the 17th century, the enlightened atheism of the 18th century, and the Victorian agnosticism of the last age. Bourgeois agnostics and proletarian atheists have attacked it from all sides. It is surprising that there is anything left of it: and few people seem even to know what it is. Thus an

[1] Budget Estimates.
[2] Cf. Joad, C. E. M., *Guide to Modern Thought* (London, 1933); and *Under the Fifth Rib: An Autobiography* (London, 1932).
[3] See p. 138.
[4] The dictum is attributed to Mr. Henry Ford.

anonymous writer recently began an article on agnosticism with the words: "The essence of religion is faith, the ability to accept as a truth a hypothesis for which there is no positive evidence."[1] Or again, in *Moscow Dialogues*, Socratov says,[2] "We are rather at a loss to point to anything of a positive character in religion. If you can suggest anything positive, I shall be glad to hear it"; and the Bishop (very conveniently) replies, "Well, first of all, the Church has always stood, even in its darkest days, for law and order." The first of these writers was confusing, as is so common, theology with religion. Theology has to accept hypotheses for which there is no positive evidence, because in a system so unlikely as the universe, of which there is only one, no comparisons can be made by which to test the credibility of anything. This is no argument in favour of theology, which may or may not be a necessary evil, but on the other hand, it does not discredit religion. The second was erecting an episcopal man of straw in order to have the pleasure of hearing the opium-merchant give himself away red-handed. But the statement is not historically true; when Irenaeus, Clement, and Tertullian were alive; when Lilburne, Rainborough, and their "russet-coated captains" were riding; the Church was not on the side of law and order. Christians were able to imagine a better law and a juster order than the established system of the Roman Empire,[3] or the government of that "Man of Blood," King Charles I.

The clearest understanding of religion has been given, in my view, by the work of Rudolf Otto,[4] a German theologian, who described it as the sense of the holy. In primitive communities we see this "numinous sense" applied to all kinds of worthless objects and rites, and later incorporated in the apparatus of State government, but in the great religions of the world it forms the essential backbone of the experience of their participators. In christianity, where the ethic of love found its greatest prophets, the numinous sense has become attached to the highest conception of the relations between man and man that we know. The christian who becomes a communist does so precisely because he sees no other body of people in the world of our time who are concerned to put Christ's commands into literal

[1] New Statesman, 1934, 8, 332 (September 15th).
[2] Hecker, J., *Moscow Dialogues* (Chapman & Hall, London, 1933), p. 191.
[3] On the socialism of the Apostolic Fathers, see the essay of Charles Marson in the collective work by Tom Mann and others, *Vox Clamantium*, ed. Andrew Reid (London, 1894); and also his *God's Co-operative Society* (Longmans, Green, London, 1914).
[4] See especially Otto, R., *The Idea of the Holy* (Oxford, 1923).

execution. If for seventeen centuries the Church has tended to put allegorical constructions on the Gospels, we know that the christians of the first two centuries did not do so.

That religion has been, and largely is, "the opium of the people" is plainly undeniable. Proletarian misery in this world has been constantly lightened by promises of comfort and blessedness in the world beyond the grave, an exhortation which might come well enough from some ecclesiastical ascetic who did not spare himself, but very ill indeed from the employer of labour or the representative of the propertied classes. But the conclusion usually drawn, namely, that religion could have no place in a socialist State, where no class-distinctions existed, does not seem to follow. Because religion has been often used as a social opiate in the past, there seems no reason why this should be so in the future. "Religion would continue to exist," writes A. L. Rowse,[1] "in the socialist community, but on its own strength. It would not have the bias of the State exerted in its favour, as it has had so strongly in England up to the present, and in greater or lesser degrees in all western countries." It may indeed be said that religion is "the protest of the oppressed creature,"[2] and that therefore when social oppression, in the form of the class-stratified society, is done away with, the private need for religion will vanish as well as the class which profited by it. This, however, is to forget what we could call "cosmic oppression," or creatureliness, the un-escapable inclusion of man in space-time, subject to pain, sorrow, sadness and death. Shall we substitute for the opium of religion an opium of science? It has always been the tacit conviction of the social reformer and the person occupied with the practical application of scientific knowledge that by man's own efforts, not merely minor evils, but the major evils of existence may be overcome. This is expressed in that great sentence: "Philosophers have talked about the universe enough; the time has come to change it."[3] But the problem of evil is not capable of so simple a resolution. So long as time continues, so long as change and decay are around us and in us, so long will sorrow and tragedy be with us.[4] "Life is a sad composition," as

---

[1] Rowse, A. L., *Politics and the Younger Generation* (Faber, London, 1931), p. 194.

[2] Marx, K., *Introduction to a Critique of Hegel's Philosophy of Law.*

[3] And also in the great concluding paragraph of John Stuart Mill's *On Liberty* (written between 1854 and 1859).

[4] Cf. Kierkegaard's distinction between "tribulations" (natural troubles which can only be endured) and "temptations" (troubles due to, and soluble by, acts of will), discussed by Auden in *New Year Letter*, 1941, p. 132.

Sir Thomas Browne said, "we live with death and die not in a moment." Or, in the words of the *Contakion*, "For so thou didst ordain when thou createdst us, saying, 'Dust thou art, and unto dust shalt thou return'; wherefore all we who go down into the grave make our song unto thee, sighing and saying, Give rest, O Christ, to thy servants with thy saints, where sorrow and sighing are no more, neither pain, but life everlasting." The whole realm of thought and feeling embodied in these phrases is fundamentally natural and proper to man, and there is little to be gained by trying to replace it by a eupeptic opium, derived from too bright an estimate of the possibilities of scientific knowledge. Driven out, it will return in the end with redoubled force.

Fundamentally natural and proper to man, the sense of the holy is as appropriate to him as the sense of beauty. As we have seen, the "moral theology" of communism lacks a doctrine of God, but this does not affect the existence of the sense of the holy. After all, the theology of the Gospels was not very complicated—Jesus did not meet disease and hunger by persuading people that blessedness was already theirs if they would accept a dogmatic intellectual system; but by curing sickness and distributing bread. This was the practical aspect of his teaching about love. In the motives of atheist communists we detect, therefore, that which is worthy of numinous respect, for they are working to bring in the World Co-operative Commonwealth.

Those who deny the importance of the sense of the holy are in an analogous position to those who cannot appreciate music or painting. It is an attitude towards the universe, an attitude almost of respect, for which nothing can be substituted. "The problem of death," it has been said,[1] "is not a 'problem' at all, it is due simply to the clash between an idealistic egoistic philosophy and the disappearance of the individual, not in the least to the fact of death." On this epicurean view, science reveals facts to us so clearly as to reconcile us to them.[2] But it is not our own death that we are thinking of. We may well be content to live on only in the effects which our living has produced on our generation and those that come after.[3] The point is that no matter now much we know in the classless State about the biology of death, we shall still suffer when someone that we have loved

---

[1] Pascal, R., Outpost, 1932, **1**, 70.

[2] All sciences have as their aim the transformation of tribulations into temptations, Auden, loc. cit. But the process is asymptotic.

[3] A point of view admirably put in Afinogenov's play *Distant Point*.

suddenly dies or is killed. The question then reduces itself to a matter of taste; shall we bury him with unloving haste and a callous reference to the unimportance of the individual? Or shall we remember, as we fulfil the rites of a liturgical requiem, that this is the common end of all the sons of men, and so unite ourselves with the blessed company of all faithful people, those who earnestly looked and worked in their generation for the coming of the Kingdom? It is true indeed, as Merejkovsky has said, that whether we believe in Christ or not, we must certainly suffer with him. And, indeed, it is my opinion that if the ancient christian modes of satisfying this numinous sense are discontinued (Eliot's *"vieilles usines désaffectés"*), other liturgical forms will be devised to play their part in attempting to express that which cannot be expressed. This we already see in such cases as the tomb of Lenin himself, and the Red Corners.

In the Timiriazev Institute at Moscow I examined the red banner which the scientists there were accustomed to carry on May Day and other public occasions. It was of a velvety cloth with yellow fringes and an elaborate hammer and sickle. How tawdry some of our respectable middle class people in England would have thought it. How they despise the native decorations and pictures on British Trade Union banners on the rare occasions when these pass through the streets in the light of day. But to me it was quite clearly numinous, one with the cross of our salvation and the *Vexilla Regis* indeed, conspicuous in the vanguard of humanity moving from the captivity of necessity into the glorious liberty of the children of God. But is this process ever complete? Are we not all for ever in bondage to space-time? Is not this bondage our final evil? It is absurd to say that "with the denial of an objective creator, socialism forgets the problem of evil." Certainly no "person" is now responsible, but in whatever society man arranges himself he must take up some attitude towards the universe, and to the fate of individuals in it, and in this attitude, the sense of the holy will always be an element.

Scientific Opium.

Not to be awake to the iniquity of class oppression, then, is religious opium. Scientific opium would mean not being awake to the tragic side of life, to the numinous elements of the world and of human effort in the world, to religious worship. Scientific opium has often been thought an integral part of marxism by its opponents, but for us the question is what break with tradition the contribution of

England and the west of Europe to the socialisation of the world must involve. In this connection there are two considerations which seem relevant, but which have not often been discussed. In the first place, it is a historical coincidence that the early marxists adopted the anthropological and psychological arguments against religion which were fashionable at the time. These arguments are insufficient ground for condemning one of the greatest forms of human experience. The anthropological arguments all confuse origin with value, as if primitive barbarism were not in the end responsible for science, art, and literature just as much as for religion. To say that the concept of God is derived from, or modelled on, the relation of primitive exploiting lord to primitive exploited slave is to say nothing about the religious value of the concept in a society where exploitation has been abolished (should it continue to exist there); still less about religion itself as opposed to theology or philosophy. For religion does not know what God is; it only knows him if he exists to be worthy of worship—a God comprehended would be no God—and it does not know why the universe is as it is, but only that there is holiness in it. An excess of mystical religion may indeed engender an attitude of inactivity against the external world, but we need it as a salt, not a whole diet. Must we have prohibition in the classless State because some men drink too deeply to-day? In the end, there is but one end, and communism can overcome the last enemy no more than any other of man's devices. It is difficult, no doubt, to combine scientific "pride" with religious "humility," but the best things often are difficult.

In the second place, the Byzantine nature of eastern christianity is relevant. From the very beginning the Byzantine Church showed a speculative rather than a practical tendency.[1] The east enacted creeds, the west discipline. The first decree of an eastern council was to determine the relations of the Godhead; the first decree of the Bishop of Rome was to prohibit the marriage of the clergy. Eastern theology was rhetorical in form and based on philosophy; western theology was logical in form and based on law. The Byzantine divine succeeded to the place of the Greek sophist; the Latin divine to the place of the Roman advocate. The eastern Church, therefore, occupied with philosophy and theology, made little or no pretensions to control of economic affairs, no attempt to subordinate the secular power to

[1] See Milman, H. H., *History of Latin Christianity* (Murray, London, 1867); and Stanley, A. P., *Lectures on the History of the Eastern Church* (Dent, Everyman edition).

itself in the interests of a particular theory as to how the mercantile life should be lived. The Patriarchs, chosen from a monastic order remarkable for its detachment from secular business, left all economic questions to the chamberlains and officials who thronged the imperial court. After the fall of Byzantium, this same tradition of complete other-worldliness transferred itself to the Church of Russia. The Russian Orthodox Church had no pope, no Hildebrand, to impose a theological system of economics on Russian society. It had no scholastic philosophers, no "mediaeval clerks" to dictate to kings and rulers what measures they should take to secure social justice. It had nothing corresponding to our 17th-century High Churchmen, or to our 19th-century Anglo-Catholics, reviving those traditions and reminding men of the ideals of a pre-capitalist age. When capitalism, in the time of Peter the Great, reached Russia, it found a perfectly virgin soil for its operations, and had no such uphill task as it found in the west. In three generations it enslaved a population which could make no appeal to any distinctively christian social theories. The appeal would have been vain, for the Orthodox Church had no such theories, and had never developed the first beginnings of them. On the contrary, it had become completely identified with the process of exploitation of the Russian people. The contrast between this situation and our own is quite remarkable.

It may be said that the meaning of the phrase "religious opium" was that by anaesthetising the people, it prevented them from performing those social actions necessary for social progress, combining in unions, rebelling against exploitation, fighting the possessing class in every possible way. "Scientific opium" could have no such meaning. Yet I think it has, and it may be explained as follows. It is a blindness to the suffering of others. A certain degree of ruthlessness is absolutely inevitable in the period of revolutions when the people are defending themselves against the final attack of the possessing class which sees itself on the verge of expropriation. "Revolutions," said Lenin, "cannot be made without breaking heads." But just as Lunacharsky (whose role will be better appreciated by later historians) pleaded successfully for the preservation of certain buildings, art treasures, etc. in the heat of the revolution; so it is always necessary for the christian man (even he who without reservation allies himself with the revolution) to plead for the retention of certain christian principles in dealing with people. The ruthlessness necessary in a revolutionary period or an age of wars may too easily pass over, especially in a

69

society based on science, and the more so the more it is so based, into a ruthlessness derived from the very statistical character of the scientific method itself. The ruthlessness with which a biologist throws out an anomalous embryo useless for his immediate purpose, the ruthlessness with which an astronomer rejects an aberrant observation, may too easily be applied to human misfits and deviationists in the socialist world order. The witness of the christian man may then recall the marxist to a sense of the fundamentally unmarxist character of such treatment. It is unmarxist because no philosophy recognises the emergence of levels of high organisation better than dialectical materialism, and the individuals of which the human social collectivity is built up are themselves the most complicated organisms in the living world.[1] Hence christian love in the form of tolerance is transformed into a recognition of the manifold forms which human thought and being may take. As long as aberrant individuals are not permitted to be a danger to the socialist state, the greatest tolerance should prevail. There is no need for marxists to follow the example of those many unchristian christians who manned the Inquisition, the witch-hunting tribunals, and the boards of godly divines in Geneva, Westminster and Massachusetts.

We have here a principle of genuine importance. Christian theology has been called "the grandmother of bolshevism," since communist planning alone has seen how to incorporate the love of one's fellow-men in the actual structure of economic life. Some have seen another ancestor in the rationalist and philanthropic ethic of ancient confucianism. But communism is based just as much on the findings of natural science and the method of science itself. The socialist society must therefore guard against taking over from science too much of scientific abstraction, scientific statistical ruthlessness, and scientific detachment from the individual.

Christian Theology the Grandmother of Bolshevism.

Important for the decay of religion in our time is the general and increasing domination of the scientific mind, or, rather, of a popular version of the state of mind characteristic of the scientific worker. Constantly growing power over external nature leads to a tacit belief in the possibility of solving the problem of evil by what might almost be called a matter of engineering. The principle of abstraction leads to a weakening of that attention to the individual and the unique

[1] This explains Blake's antipathy to Newton.

which must always be an integral part of the religious outlook. The principle of ethical neutrality leads to a general chaos in the traditional systems of morals, and hence to decay in the religious emotion formerly attached to the performance of certain actions. The emphasis laid by the scientific mentality on the quantitative aspects of nature runs diametrically counter to the emphasis which religion would like to lay on the other aspects of the universe. And, above all, in actively interfering with the external world, in persistently probing its darkest corners, science destroys that feeling of creaturely dependence upon, and intimate relation to, a transcendent and supernal Being, which has certainly been one of the most marked characteristics of the religious spirit. In the modern world, Epicurus and Lucretius have come into their own.

But here we find, paradoxically enough, that communism and the christian religion are again on the same side. If these effects of the domination of science were to operate alone, we should have a truly soulless society, much as is depicted by Bertrand Russell in *The Scientific Outlook*,[1] and by Aldous Huxley, satirically, in *Brave New World*.[2] This is what we shall certainly get if capitalism can establish itself anew and overcome the forces of fanatical nationalism which threaten to disrupt it. For capitalism has a fundamentally cheap estimate of the value of human life; mine disasters and wars alike are but passing incidents in a society where the only principle recognised is that might is right. Communism and christianity, on the contrary, estimate life highly. Ultimately the distinction here resolves itself into what kind of human society we wish to aim at, and the choice may be in a sense aesthetic. The logical continuation of the capitalist order would be the tightening and stabilisation of class-stratification, which seems to be the essential function of fascism. This could then, in time, be further fixed as biological engineering becomes more powerful. In such a civilisation, the Utopia of the bourgeoisie, where an abundance of docile workers of very limited intelligence was available, the class stratification would be absolute, and the governing class alone would be capable of living anything approaching a full life.[3] Biological engineering would have done what mechanical engineering had failed

---

[1] (Allen & Unwin, London, 1931.)

[2] (Chatto & Windus, London, 1932.) We shall analyse this book in what follows.

[3] It is of much interest that the similarity between fascism and the ancient caste-system of India is expressly admitted in *Sanatana Dharma*, an advanced textbook of Hindu religion and ethics, published by the Central Hindu College, Benares, 1923, pp. 240 ff. Both are said to be based on the doctrine of immortality.

to do, and flesh and blood would have been adapted to machinery rather than machinery to flesh and blood. Nevertheless the converse process is equally possible, i.e. a continually increasing automatism of machine operations, and hence an increasing liberation of man from the necessity of productive labour. With the increase of leisure would come an enormous increase in the beneficial and pleasurable occupations available for the workers. This is what is meant by the readiness to sacrifice the bourgeois liberty of to-day for the much greater liberty of the classless State. And these two alternatives are even now offering themselves to us, with capitalism on the one side and christianity and communism together on the other. It is a pity that Spengler's aphorism is not more widely known: "Christian theology is the grandmother of bolshevism."

"Utopias," wrote Berdyaev, in a passage which Aldous Huxley chose for the motto of *Brave New World*," appear to be much more realisable than we used to think. We are finding ourselves face to face with a far more awful question—how can we avoid their actualisation? And perhaps a new period is beginning, a period when intelligent men will be wondering how they can avoid these Utopias, and return to a society non-Utopian, less perfect but more free." Huxley's book was a brilliant commentary on this.

His theme is twofold, one of its aspects being the power of autocratic dictatorship, and the other, the possibilities of this power, given the resources of a really advanced biological engineering. The book opens with a long description of a human embryo factory, where the eggs emitted by carefully-tended ovaries are brought up in their development by mass-production methods on an endless conveyor belt moving very slowly until at last the infants are "decanted" one by one into a remarkable world. The methods of education by continual suggestion and all the possibilities of conditional reflexes are brilliantly described, and we see a world where art and religion no longer exist, but in which an absolutely stable form of society has been achieved, first by sorting out the eggs into groups of known inherited characteristics and then setting each group when adult to do the work for which it is fitted; and secondly by allowing unlimited sexual life (of course, sterile). This idea was based on the suggestion of Kyrle[1] that social discontent, which has always been an important driving force in social change, is a manifestation of the Oedipus complexes of the members of society and cannot be removed by

[1] R. M. Kyrle, Psyche, 1931, 11, 48.

economic means. With decrease of sexual tabus, these psychologists suggest, there would be a decrease of frustration and hence of that aggressiveness which finds its sublimation in religion or its outlet in political activity. Thus in the society pictured by Aldous Huxley, erotic play of children is encouraged rather than prevented, universal but superficial sex relations are the rule, and indeed any sign of the beginning of more deep and lasting affection is stamped out as being anti-social.

Perhaps only biologists really appreciated the full force of *Brave New World*. They knew that Huxley included nothing in his book but what might be considered legitimate extrapolations from already existing knowledge and power. Successful experiments are even now being made in the cultivation of embryos of small mammals *in vitro*. One of the most horrible of Huxley's predictions, the production of numerous workers of low-grade intelligence and precisely identical genetic constitution from one egg, is theoretically quite possible. Armadillos, parasitic insects, and even sea-urchins, if treated in the right manner, will "bud" in this way now, and the difficulties in the way of effecting it with mammalian and therefore human eggs are probably purely technical.

It is just the same in the realm of philosophy. There are already among us tendencies leading in the direction of Huxley's realm of Antichrist. Fascism seeks no justification other than existence and force. Its philosophy is one in which there is no place for science. Science ceases to be the groundwork of philosophy, and becomes nothing but the mythology accompanying a technique. Divorced from religion, ethics and art, as well as from philosophy, it proceeds to do the will of wicked and ungodly rulers upon humanity. "The scientific society in its pure form," as Bertrand Russell has said, "is incompatible with the pursuit of truth, with love, with art, with spontaneous delight, with every ideal that men have hitherto cherished, save only possibly ascetic renunciation. It is not knowledge that is the source of these dangers. Knowledge is good and ignorance is evil—to this principle the lover of the world can admit no exception. Nor is it power in and for itself that is the source of danger. What is dangerous is power wielded for the sake of power, not power wielded for the sake of genuine good."

This train of thought leads us finally to consider on what ground communism can stand as against nietzschianism or other doctrines of the "superman." These may be, for all we know, perennial, if they derive primarily from specific psychological types, and may appear long after the classless society has been established. Thus if it be claimed that the fulfilment of the personality of one sort of individual necessitates the injury or exploitation of others, on what ground does communist theory refute the claim? The ethical superiority of social equality is in fact at issue. Barbara Wootton[1] well points out that "every type of economic organisation will turn top-heavy unless it is quite definitely and deliberately weighted in favour of the weak, the unfortunate, and the incompetent." What justification can there be for this, except the ἀγαπή τοῦ πλησίου of the Gospels, one of the two commandments on which hang all the Law and the Prophets? And this leads us to ask whence came the noble hatred of oppression found in Marx, and whence arises this passion in all the communist confessors and martyrs of the present century? It cannot be a coincidence that marxist morality grew up in the bosom of christianity after eighteen christian centuries, as if the phoenix of the Kingdom should arise from the ashes of the Church's failure.

---

[1] *Plan or No Plan* (Gollancz, London, 1934), p. 106.

THE LITERATURE OF
DEATH AND DYING

Abrahamsson, Hans. **The Origin of Death:** Studies in African Mythology. 1951

Alden, Timothy. **A Collection of American Epitaphs and Inscriptions with Occasional Notes.** Five vols. in two. 1814

Austin, Mary. **Experiences Facing Death.** 1931

Bacon, Francis. **The Historie of Life and Death with Observations Naturall and Experimentall for the Prolongation of Life.** 1638

Barth, Karl. **The Resurrection of the Dead.** 1933

Bataille, Georges. **Death and Sensuality:** A Study of Eroticism and the Taboo. 1962

Bichat, [Marie François] Xavier. **Physiological Researches on Life and Death.** 1827

Browne, Thomas. **Hydriotaphia.** 1927

Carrington, Hereward. **Death:** Its Causes and Phenomena with Special Reference to Immortality. 1921

Comper, Frances M. M., editor. **The Book of the Craft of Dying and Other Early English Tracts Concerning Death.** 1917

Death and the Visual Arts. 1976

Death as a Speculative Theme in Religious, Scientific, and Social Thought. 1976

Donne, John. **Biathanatos.** 1930

Farber, Maurice L. **Theory of Suicide.** 1968

Fechner, Gustav Theodor. **The Little Book of Life After Death.** 1904

Frazer, James George. **The Fear of the Dead in Primitive Religion.** Three vols. in one. 1933/1934/1936

Fulton, Robert. **A Bibliography on Death, Grief and Bereavement:** 1845-1975. 1976

Gorer, Geoffrey. **Death, Grief, and Mourning.** 1965

Gruman, Gerald J. **A History of Ideas About the Prolongation of Life.** 1966

Henry, Andrew F. and James F. Short, Jr. **Suicide and Homicide.** 1954

Howells, W[illiam] D[ean], et al. **In After Days;** Thoughts on the Future Life. 1910

Irion, Paul E. **The Funeral:** Vestige or Value? 1966

Landsberg, Paul-Louis. **The Experience of Death:** The Moral Problem of Suicide. 1953

Maeterlinck, Maurice. **Before the Great Silence.** 1937

Maeterlinck, Maurice. **Death.** 1912

Metchnikoff, Élie. **The Nature of Man:** Studies in Optimistic Philosophy. 1910

Metchnikoff, Élie. **The Prolongation of Life:** Optimistic Studies. 1908

Munk, William. **Euthanasia.** 1887

Osler, William. **Science and Immortality.** 1904

Return to Life: Two Imaginings of the Lazarus Theme. 1976

Stephens, C[harles] A[sbury]. **Natural Salvation:** The Message of Science. 1905

Sulzberger, Cyrus. **My Brother Death.** 1961

Taylor, Jeremy. **The Rule and Exercises of Holy Dying.** 1819

Walker, G[eorge] A[lfred]. **Gatherings from Graveyards.** 1839

Warthin, Aldred Scott. **The Physician of the Dance of Death.** 1931

Whiter, Walter. **Dissertation on the Disorder of Death.** 1819

Whyte, Florence. **The Dance of Death in Spain and Catalonia.** 1931

Wolfenstein, Martha. **Disaster:** A Psychological Essay. 1957

Worcester, Alfred. **The Care of the Aged, the Dying, and the Dead.** 1950

Zandee, J[an]. **Death as an Enemy According to Ancient Egyptian Conceptions.** 1960

090197